# ECONOMIC GOVERNMENT

# ECONOMIC GOVERNMENT

*Robert Klassen*

Writers Club Press

San Jose New York Lincoln Shanghai

# Economic Government

Writers Club Press
an imprint of iUniverse.com, Inc.

For information address:
iUniverse.com, Inc.
5220 S 16th, Ste. 200
Lincoln, NE 68512
www.iuniverse.com

ISBN: 0-595-17403-5

Printed in the United States of America

*With humility I dedicate this work to Homo Sapiens*

# Contents

*Space Age Technology Ruled by Dark Age Paradigms
Means Extinction*

# Acknowledgements

I learned from Andrew J. Galambos in 1972 that ideas are property, then later I read the same thing written in the 1947 history, *Across the Wide Missouri*, by Bernard DeVoto. In 1973 I learned from Galambos that insurance can represent a model for government, then later I read the same thing written in the 1852 book, *An Essay on The Trial by Jury*, by Lysander Spooner. A scholar would undoubtedly labor to unearth the origins of the ideas that I work with in my writing; unfortunately, I am not a scholar, so I cannot cite sources item by item. However, I can and do enthusiastically thank those people who have taught me about government over the years, beginning with Henry David Thoreau, my earliest teacher, then Ayn Rand, and finally, Mr. Galambos. This short list leaves out hundreds of writers and thinkers who have contributed to my general fund of knowledge, but since this book is confined to the subject of government, I'll leave it at that. I would particularly recommend reading Thoreau's *Civil Disobedience,* Rand's *Atlas Shrugged,* and Galambos' *Sic Itur ad Astra.*

# Introduction

I believe that government itself is a natural phenomenon among social species, that is species whose individual members prefer to live in close proximity to one another, like prairie dogs, elephants, wolves, dolphins, ants, and Homo Sapiens. We may observe that each species lives in some kind of social organization that enables it to survive. From our observations we infer that a given species' social organization is somehow natural or instinctual, that it is not deliberately thought out or planned and agreed upon by individual members and then carried out; indeed, it may be hard-wired into each individual nervous system so that survival tasks are carried out automatically. We do not believe that this is the case in Homo Sapiens; we do believe that individual members of our species have thought out and planned our social organization in advance and that we all have more or less have agreed to it.

I wonder about that. What is the nature of Homo Sapiens? When Raymond Dart, the Australian physical anthropologist and paleontologist who discovered Australopithecus africanus, first revealed his speculations about how the little skulls of our ancestors may have been fractured in such an unusual way, his ideas were greeted with an international storm of denial; surely our ancestors were not killers! Mountains of subsequent evidence indicate that they were. I think we can safely presume that the deliberate use of physical force is embedded in human nature.

It did not surprise me to learn that the first "cities" that Homo Sapiens built were crude fortifications (Sumer, Akkad, Jericho) built around water holes or wells. We don't know what kind of social organization prevailed in those forts ten-thousand years ago, but again I think we can safely presume that the later models of Crete, Mycenea, and Troy demonstrate that the deliberate use of physical force to organize society came naturally to our species from the very beginning.

My thesis is that we have gone about as far as we can go with this natural model of social organization and that to persist in the use of force will lead to the self-extinction of our species. We don't have to presume anything about what happened during the last century, we know it for a fact. Our science and technology put unprecedented physical force into the hands of political governments that used it to murder one-hundred-and-seventy-million people. Today nuclear bombs abound around the planet and nuclear winter awaits a single command. What trend in the history of political government encourages me to believe that no man will use that power and give that command? None that I can find. It's only a matter of time.

While we have that time, I think we should use it to explore other methods of organizing society that put the use of force at extreme disadvantage and that could eventually render this natural human tendency ineffective and harmless. There are other models for government. There is the privately owned, proprietary cruise ship model where every passenger is either a paying customer or a contracted employee of the owning company. There is the privately owned, proprietary city model that I describe in my book, *Atlantis: A Novel about Economic Government*. There is the shopping mall model and the free-port model, both described by Spencer MacCallum, which I discuss later. I have lumped these models into a single concept that I call economic government, where the proper functions of government, security and justice, are available for sale in a free-market backed by a simple money-back guarantee of satisfaction. The use of physical force is not only not necessary in economic government, it is an absolute impediment to survival in society, the polar opposite of what we get in political government.

This economic paradigm for government has never been tried. We have always relied on the use of force to organize society, so to imagine some other way of doing things is very difficult. I will try to look at the potentials of economic government to correct the failures and to ameliorate the threats of political government as a method of organizing society that could endure without the use of force.

# Economic Government

## 1998

### Written in gratitude to the ideas of Ayn Rand and Andrew J. Galambos.

Recently I had a very long-winded discussion with my sister's friend Alicia Travest on the subject of economic government. Alicia is a skeptical person who neither likes me nor trusts me, plus she is a well educated and intelligent person who enjoys asking insightful and difficult questions, so I decided that this whole conversation needed to be written down and saved for posterity. For the sake of brevity, Alicia will be A and I will be B.

A: Okay, mister, what is this? I've heard of economics and I've heard of politics and I've heard of political-economy, but I've never heard of economic government.

B: Relax. I'll tell you about it. I coined the phrase—economic government—deliberately in order to clearly contrast it with what we have now, which I call political government.

A: Wait a minute, you made this up?

B: Yes, I put the two words side-by-side.

A: Have you got a degree in economics or political-science?

B: I haven't got a degree in anything.

A: Then by what right...

B: The same right every person has to learn and to think and to arrive at conclusions.

A: How long have you been studying this?

B: Since I read *Civil Disobedience* at the age of ten in 1950.

A: Who wrote that?

B: Henry David Thoreau, in 1849. The essay begins: "I heartily accept the motto, 'That government is best which governs least'; and I should like to see it acted up to more rapidly and systematically. Carried out, it amounts to this, which also I believe—'That government is best which governs not at all'; and when men are prepared for it, that will be the kind of government which they will have."

A: So are you saying that economic government is no government at all?

B: No. Thoreau was using the word *govern* in the sense of *rule by authority*. He did not like the idea of being ruled by anybody other than himself and he refused to acknowledge the authority of the state. However, *govern* also means *to exercise influence*, which is not the same thing as ruling by threat, command, or demand. It is in this sense that I am using the word *government*.

A: So by attaching your use of the word to economics, you are implying that economics can somehow exercise influence over what?

B: Human behavior. The purpose of economic government is to provide absolute security and justice to individuals without the use of coercion.

A: What do you mean by coercion?

B: Any interference with property.

A: You mean force, right? So you're going to influence human behavior without the threat of force? You're crazier than I thought. Force is the only way to keep people in line.

B: So when you move to a job that pays twice as much, somebody forced you to do it?

A: No, no, you know what I mean.

B: You act on your self-interest, right? Nobody has to force you to do that, right?

A: So what? What about muggers and rapists and thieves and killers and all those people? What do you do with them?

B: Life will become very unpleasant for them in this system. In fact, I don't believe they will be able to carry out a coercive act and survive. As the news gets around, I do believe this kind of behavior will become rare, indeed. In economic government, coercers will *pay* for their crimes.

A: I don't like the way you said that and I definitely don't like the grin on your face. Okay, let's get down to business, what is this economic government of yours?

B: It consists of three interrelated human institutions that do not exist at the moment. First, and most important, is an *Innovation Clearinghouse*, second is *Banking*, and third is *Insurance*.

A: Who are you trying to kid, here? Banking and insurance have been around forever.

B: Banking and insurance have been around in rudimentary form, but their function has never been extended as it ought to be. In fact, such extensions are most likely illegal under political government.

A: Illegal, you say? Now you've got me interested. Like what, for instance?

B: How about venture-capital insurance?

A: Like you bet your money on a risky venture and loose your shirt and the insurance company picks up the tab. Right?

B: Right. Then there's marriage insurance and contract insurance and innovation insurance…

A: There you go with that innovation business again. What's wrong with patents and copyrights?

B: Patents are expensive and difficult to get; then, if they are worth anything, even more expensive and difficult to protect. Patents also discourage innovation and competition. Copyrights are cheap and easy to get, all you have to do is write the word on the page, but are also expensive and difficult to protect. And both have time limits.

A: I suppose you have something better?

B: Yes, the Innovation Clearinghouse. It begins with a simple registry where you can list your innovation and have it time and date stamped.

A: Won't that make it easier to steal?

B: You can encrypt it.

A: What if it's something I create while I'm working for somebody else?

B: Then you'd better encrypt your name as well.

A: How much does it cost?

B: Very little, maybe one cent per entry.

A: Well, that's cheap enough, but I still don't know why I should do it in the first place.

B: The broader function of the Clearinghouse is to create a tree of knowledge to identify each individual innovator who belongs on that tree. Then the Clearinghouse will accept royalties from entrepreneurs who have used those innovations to earn a profit and assign those royalties to the innovators.

A: Whoa! Wait just a hot minute here. That tree of knowledge could go back ten-thousand years!

B: Further, actually. We have the inventors of the wheel, inventors of stone tools...

A: This is ridiculous! You can't pay people who have been dead for thousands of years.

B: You can't pay the person, but you can create an account for that person and pay into that.

A: What on earth for? I'd like to know.

B: First, because you're using somebody else's property. If you use the knowledge that some other person created to earn a profit for yourself, then you owe that person. Second, you will build up investments that earn money that can be used for education, research, and development of new knowledge. And third, it is a tool of justice.

A: Slow down, slow down. Let me examine these one at a time. Are you telling me that every mechanical engineer is going to have to learn and remember the names of thousands of people who created his profession?

B: No, not at all. If the mechanical engineer is merely contracting his time to do a certain job, then he doesn't owe money to anybody. If he is building his own hydraulic pumps and selling them to an aerospace company at a profit, then he does. He does not need to know or remember his antecedents, the Clearinghouse will take care of that.

A: I still don't see what's in it for him?

B: For one thing, he can advertise the fact that he pays innovation royalties, thus attracting the highest quality co-contractors to his projects. And for another, he himself will eventually earn innovation royalties as others build upon his work, even after he is dead, so participating in the Innovation Clearinghouse is in his own best interest.

A: Who's to say this Clearinghouse won't steal his money or his innovation or both?

B: That is the purpose of innovation insurance.

A: Is this Clearinghouse one great enormous institution?

B: Not necessarily, there may be thousands, but they will be interrelated like the search engines and directories on the Internet are now.

A: Okay, I get the picture. Now what did you say they do with the money?

B: Invest it in profitable businesses, invest it in individuals with profitable potential, and invest it in research and development of areas which have no apparent application at the moment.

A: I can see the point of the first two, they'll earn money on their investment, but what is the point of the third?

B: Looking back, we see a phenomenon like Maxwell's Equations explaining something that was not known to exist, electromagnetic waves. Today the search is on for the gravitational waves that Einstein predicted. Today the search is on to find new medicines in the tropical forests. Somebody has to finance this research, which may or may not pay for itself some day. Individuals or corporations may pay for it, fine, but the Innovation Clearinghouse will take a keen interest in pure research.

A: Okay, okay. Back up a little and tell me what this Clearinghouse has to do with justice.

B: In addition to recording and rewarding the positive acts of individuals, the Innovation Clearinghouse will also record and punish the negative acts of individuals.

A: I can't believe you are saying this. How can you punish dead people?

B: Two ways; one, by publishing their negative act; and two, by creating a negative account in their name. Men like Stalin and Hitler would have pretty substantial negative balances.

A: What on earth for?

B: Because these people have destroyed property and because it will have a real deterrent effect on any would-be Hitlers or Stalins in the future.

A: And you're going to take that back in history, too?

B: Sure. The murder of Archimedes cries out for justice. We may believe that a delay of two and a third millennia makes the punishment irrelevant, but to the folks living a hundred-thousand years from now, it will appear instantaneous.

A: You think big, don't you? Why should I care what they think in a hundred-thousand years?

B: Because, if you do anything worthwhile in the time you've got, they will be there to thank you. If you don't, they won't.

A: Is that a threat?

B: No, it's more like a guarantee. Every political government in the history of mankind has turned its monopoly on coercion against its own citizens in its attempt to enslave them, or to keep them enslaved, which ultimately destroyed not only the political government but also the civilization that supported it. I perceive history as the rise and fall of one Dark Age after another. We live on the threshold of another one, only this time the technology of coercion is so sophisticated and so powerful that only a mutated version of Homo Sapiens will survive, if any version survives. We have the technical ability to destroy all life on this planet and that technology is controlled by the wrong people.

A: Who should control it?

B: The innovators.

A: How can they?

B: They can't, at the moment. When innovation insurance becomes available, that will become a different matter.

A: Economic government can save the human race?

B: Yes.

A: How?

B: By making the exercise of coercion nearly impossible.

A: And your Clearinghouse will do this?

B: Not alone, don't forget insurance and banking.

A: Okay, let's talk about insurance.

B: Any perceived act of coercion will be reported to the victim's insurance, which will verify the incident, then pay the victim the agreed-upon indemnity. Insurance then notifies the Clearinghouse and the bank, then seeks to recover the indemnity and damages from the perpetrator.

A: Wait a minute. What if the crook has insured himself against the risk beforehand?

B: This makes things simpler. Insurance X goes to Insurance Y, reveals the evidence against the crook, then collects the indemnity and damages.

A: Hold it, what happens to the crook?

B: Well, he's going to have a hard time buying new insurance and he's going to have a permanent blot on his historical record.

A: There is something missing here. What if he didn't have insurance in the first place and what if he murdered you?

B: I have insured myself against this risk, of course, so my estate is protected. The murderer can't use the banking system any longer, the banks have frozen his accounts, so he can't buy anything, food, shelter, clothing, heating, cooling, electricity, plumbing, transportation, nothing.

A: What if he stored up a horde of gold?

B: Gold is only worth what the market will pay for it. In a totally electronic banking and finance system, there will be little market for gold. Sellers of goods and services will not even accept it. It's too heavy, too bulky, and the only use for it is in teeth and jewelry and electronics.

A: So you see the banking industry going on-line?

B: Certainly. It's only logical and it's only a matter of time before all currencies and trading will be electronic.

A: That's going to leave a lot of people who are not wired out in the cold.

B: Why? People learned to use credit cards easily enough, now they can learn to use debit cards. A stolen debit card won't work for the thief.

A: So what happened to our murderer?

B: That is up to him. He can negotiate with the insurance and banking people to pay for the indemnity and damages or he can walk out into the wilderness and try to live off the land. Maybe some tribe of like-minded savages will take him in; or maybe they will eat him. In an interstellar space vehicle, that would be a life or death choice.

A: What if he saved up enough money in advance to pay for murdering you?

B: I would have to see to it in advance that murdering me would be a very expensive act. Insure against the risk. If I think I am at risk, then it's up to me to protect my property with insurance. Then the insurance company becomes very interested in protecting my property too. But if the criminal can afford to pay for his crime in advance, he still has his damaged reputation to deal with. Who would want to do business with him?

A: There's got to be a loophole here, somewhere.

B: At first there's nothing but loopholes, but as time goes on, they will be closed, one by one. As more and more people freely buy into economic government, coercion will begin to disappear.

A: And that is your objective.

B: Yes. My objective is to put an end to coercion as viable human behavior.

(Author's note: I don't have a sister.)

# Criminal Justice: A Brief Summary

### 1998

**Written with gratitude to the ideas of Andrew J. Galambos**

Two principles are the foundation of Justice in Economic Government, to reward innovation and to punish coercion.

Justice in economic government is economic. Criminal Justice is administered by insurance companies and is applied by businesses in general.

Insurance today is not understood in the sense that we are applying the concept. Insurance should be universally available throughout the planet and beyond to cover every risk that can be imagined, including the risk of coercive attack on a person's life, innovations, or tangible property. This concept of justice takes this availability for granted. This concept of justice can, however, be applied in a more limited environment, such as a proprietary city on land or a proprietary ship at sea or a proprietary vehicle in space.

Part of the function of insurance companies would have to include arbitration which is guaranteed to be neutral, that is, supplied with a money-back guarantee of neutrality. If neutrality is seen as a risk, insure against it.

The first step a victim of coercion takes is to notify his or her insurance company. The insurance company examines the facts, determines the loss, pays the victim the indemnity, and then seeks out the perpetrator.

Assuming the perpetrator has insurance, the two or more insurance companies involved arbitrate the case and determine the financial restitution and damages, exchange the appropriate funds, and the case is closed.

The coercive act is not secret, however. It is carefully recorded and published for all to see.

If the perpetrator is not insured and refuses to negotiate with the victim's insurance company, the company reports the facts to the banking system and the banks freeze his accounts.

Money, in EG, is electronic digital cash. Money can be exchanged anonymously, but the owner of a bank account is known to the bank.

On a proprietary ship at sea, for example, an uninsured perpetrator of a coercive act would discover that no facilities on the ship would work for him or her. This person has a simple choice, negotiate, or eventually be ejected by the ship.

Restitution and damages are not arbitrary matters decided at the whim of a judge, but are incorporated into the original contract between an individual and the insurance companies. An individual can choose to make coercion as expensive as he or she wishes. In Economic Government, the criminal pays for the crime.

# Economic Justice

**1999**

**How it Might Work**

**A Story**

**With gratitude to Unternehmer von Freiheit**

Jan 24, 2003 12:31pm
From: rjohnson@netronix.net <Signature verified>
Encrypted To: claims@allplanet.com

I am writing to report the theft of my automobile, a Fordorolla Model Mxb22, on Jan 23rd of this year. It is insured with your company for 40Kcr. Please advise me on the necessary claim procedures.

Yours,
Ronald Johnson

Jan 24, 2003 2:45pm
From: fsmythe@allplanet.com <Signature verified>
Encrypted To: rjohnson@netronix.com
Encrypted Cc: hhiggins@privateeyes.com

Dear Ronald:

I am sorry to hear about the loss of your automobile. My name is Fred Smythe and I will be your claim agent. At All Planet Insurance, we take theft very seriously. We have hired Henry Higgins of Private Eyes detective agency to assist in the investigation. Please send us a detailed description of the automobile and the circumstances of its disappearance. If you have friends or neighbors who have information about the circumstances of the disappearance of your auto that might be helpful, please provide Mr. Higgins with their names.

Please feel free to rent a car until we can settle your claim. Attached are Cr. good at most major car rentals companies for this purpose.

Thank you and we hope to settle your claim to your satisfaction as quickly as possible.

Fred Smythe

Jan 25, 2003 8:15am
From: rjohnson@netronix.com <Signature verified>
Encrypted To: fsmythe@allplanet.com; hhiggins@privateeyes.com

Folks,

Here are the details of the theft as I know them.

At 6:00 pm Jan 23rd I arrived home and parked my car on the street in the front of my house.
I took the keys in with me. No keys where hidden on the car. No one but me has a key to my auto, not even my wife.
At 10:00pm I locked up the house and did not notice the car missing.
At 12:00am My neighbor heard the sound of glass breaking. She went to investigate, but could see nothing unusual. (See her statement attached)
At 7:45am I left the house to drive to work and noticed the car missing. I noticed some broken glass on the pavement in the street.

Yours,
Ronald Johnson

Attachment:
Jan 24, 2003 7:45pm
From: hBickston@owl.com <Signature verified>
Encrypted To: rjohnson@netronix.com

My name is Henrietta Bickston and I live at 1303 Escobar Way, next door to Mr. Johnson. Yesterday afternoon he came by and said his car was stolen and had I heard any noises the night before. I said I had. About midnight I heard the sound of glass breaking and went to investigate, but didn't see anything unusual. I did not notice if his car was gone then, but it may have been. It is not unusual for Mr. Johnson's car to be gone, so I didn't think anything about it. Feel free to contact me if I can be of further assistance in this matter.

Jan 31, 2003 11:23 am
From: fsmythe@allplanet.com <Signature verified>
Encrypted To: rjohnson@netronix.com

Please find attached 40KCr in deposit-only digital-coinage, the value
of the insurance on your auto. Mr. Higgins will be investigating on our
behalf—we would appreciate your full cooperation and apologize for
the inconvenience. In the event that we find who stole your car and can
make a settlement with the insurance company of the thief, you shall
receive, per our contract, an additional 10KCr.

Feb 13, 2003 1:13 am
From: hhiggins@privateeyes.com <Signature verified>
Encrypted To: fsmythe@allplanet.com

Dear Sir:

We have found what we believe to be the remains of the R. Johnson auto. It is wrecked beyond repair, but the numbers on the engine and body match those of the insurance records. Additional clues in the car have given us a first lead on the thief. Analysis of biological matter found in the auto together with a search of recently abandoned leases lead us to an identification of which we are 95% certain. A local man, one Richard Pierce, age 22, has recently disappeared after losing his job and has recently been desperately short on money. Neighbors indicate that he was under great stress prior to his disappearance and that he talked about crime as a way to solve his money problems. While this man has a reasonable reputation with Id Services, his current situation makes him a likely suspect. I will gather further evidence for a charge, but I think we have enough to approach Id Service to see if they can track him down.

Higgins
Private Eyes Detective Agency

Feb 14, 2003 9:05 am
From: fsmythe@allplanet.com <Signature verified>
Encrypted To: inquiries@IdServices.com
Encrypted Cc: hhiggins@privateeyes.com

To Whom It May Concern:

All Planet Insurance is investigating the theft of a missing auto and have reason to suspect one Richard Pierce who has recently disappeared. He has an identity listed with your service. Before placing a formal charge against his identity, we would like to find out if you are in contact with him and whether he would grant an interview with our investigator.

Thank you,
Fred Smythe
Senior Claims Adjuster
All Planet Insurance

Feb 14, 2003 12:43 pm
From: ghanson@IdServices.com <Signature verified>
Encrypted To: fsmythe@allplanet.com, rpierce@noload.net
Encrypted Cc: hhiggins@privateeyes.com

Unfortunately, we cannot reach Mr. Pierce at this time. It is never pleasant when one of our customers is accused of theft, but we are here to protect the community by identifying just such people. Please send us details of the claim information. Traditionally, we will post the claim publicly, but the details are only available to owner of the identity until formal proceedings can take place or 60 days passes. It is our sincere hope this matter can be cleared up quickly.

Feb 15, 2003 10:45 am
M. Godfrey Hanson
Id Services, limited

From: ghanson@IdServices.com <Signature verified>
Encrypted To: fsmythe@allplanet.com
Encrypted Cc: rpierce@noload.net

Thank you for the claim information—it is now posted against the identity Richard Pierce. Under the identity contract he has 60 days to respond to the charge.

Due to reputation of All Planet and the seriousness of the accusation, all assets in accounts registered in Mr. Pierce's identity have been frozen pending resolution of this matter by arbitration or the passage of 60 days.

Under the identity contract our patrons sign we handle all charges by the arbitration rules laid down in Bardon Contract Guidelines. I note that All Planet also uses these guidelines, so we defer to the ruling of arbitration between you and Mr. Pierce unless he fails to respond in 60 days. As you know, we must remain impartial with regard to a customer's identity and have a rigid set of rules governing our ratings and procedures.

Mr. Pierce has no appropriate insurance account registered under his identity, however, the terms of the identity contract, in accordance with the general agreement between Banks, Insurance and ID services, allows us to withdraw from his account to settle the charge for arbitration and even to draw on his credit lines.

If Mr. Pierce does not answer the charge in 60 days, we will settle the claim as per the terms in the contract.

—Godfrey

Apr 26, 2003 8:14 am
From: ghanson@IdServices.com <Signature verified>
Encrypted To: fsmythe@allplanet.com

It has been 60 days since the claim against Richard Pierce was made. He has not attempted to address the charge, so we have opened his accounts. The total cash raised from balance and credit line draws is 2KCr which I have attached in deposit-only digital coinage. The balance of 48KCr is outstanding. The charges are now made public and we have assigned our lowest rating in all categories for this identity.

I have added the All Planet account to Mr. Pierce's identity, showing his current debt to your company.

—Godfrey

Oct 2, 2007 7:31 pm
To: inquries@IdServices.com <Signature verified>
From: fuzzy@wow.com

My name is Richard Pierce and I wish to reclaim my identity at Id Services. I know this is a difficult thing to do, but after living the past four years with an identity that does not extend prior to my 23 birthday, I simply must try. Getting a job with a crappy identity is almost impossible. I even tried to buy a fake ID, but it was shut down after a week—lost a lot of money doing that. I'm tired of starving; tired of living under the highway—I want something of a life and I am willing to pay to get it back.

Stealing the car was stupid—I thought I could beat the system somehow, but I couldn't sell it. No one wants to buy a car like that—it so easily traceable. When I couldn't sell it I tried to destroy it by running it off a cliff so it couldn't be traced to me, but somehow it was. Anyway stealing was wrong and it sure didn't pay. I've had my share of punishment as a result and I'm sick of running.

I would like to know what I can do to pay my debt. I know I cannot erase the charge against my name, but I have found a man who said he would give me a decent job if I came clean, so I'm coming clean.

Thank you,
Richard Pierce

Oct 3, 2007 9:12 am
From: larmey@IdServices.com <Signature verified>
Encrypted To: fuzzy@wow.com
Encrypted Cc: rpierce@noload.net, fsmythe@allplanet.com

Mr. Pierce:

Your account total is now—67KCr. due to accrued interest on your credit line to the insurance company. I've called All Planet Insurance and they have agreed to lower your interest by 3% if you agree to merge your current identity reflecting your last three or so years of records with your identity here. As you know, you cannot remove the charge from your account, but paying off your debt will raise your credit rating and improve your citizen rating. The maximum citizen rating you can ever have on this identity is a 4 (out of 10) with a record of a serious theft

—Lola

Oct 3, 2010 11:52 am
From: fsmythe@allplanet.com <Signature verified>
Encrypted To: rjohnson@netronix.com

Mr. Johnson,

Attached is 10KCr. reflecting the bonus we owe you for fully recovering the insured amount of your stolen auto. Your cooperation with the Private Eyes agency and patience has finally made this possible.

—Fred Johnson

# Innovation Clearinghouse

**1998**

**This essay is written with gratitude to the ideas of:**

**Andrew J. Galambos**
**Alvin Lowi, Jr.**
**Stephen J. Parker**
**Stephen Foerster**
**Simon Buckingham**
**Christopher Klassen**
**John Hilton**

An Innovation Clearinghouse may serve several purposes:

Innovation Directory
Innovation Registry
Innovation Agency
Innovation Justice
Innovation Insurance
Innovation Arbitration

Innovation is defined in *Webster's Ninth New Collegiate Dictionary* as *1: the introduction of something new 2: a new idea, method, or device.* I am using the word in both senses of this definition.

Clearinghouse is defined in *Webster's Ninth New Collegiate Dictionary* as *1: an establishment maintained by banks for settling mutual claims and accounts 2: a central agency for the collection, classification, and distribution esp.*(sic) *of information.* I am using the word clearinghouse in both senses of this definition.

The central, key concept of a clearinghouse for ideas is the innovation of Andrew J. Galambos, as far as I know. His intention, as I understand it, was to bring absolute justice to the innovators throughout history who made it possible for our species to survive the rigors of nature and to emerge as the dominant species on this planet. That justice consisted of finding them, naming them, thanking them, and paying them gratitude, i.e., money. This would be the function of what I am calling an Innovation Directory.

WHO PAYS: The gratitude to innovators is paid by the entrepreneur or manufacturer who produces and sells products based on that innovation. In practical terms, the entrepreneur or manufacturer would simply designate a percentage of profits, say one-one-hundredth of one percent, as gratitude and the Innovation Directory would distribute it appropriately down the tree of knowledge.

WHY PAY: Imagine the extent of human knowledge in 1650: Algebra and geometry had been recovered from the ancient Greeks; Kepler had published his Laws of Motion; Galileo had published his Law of Falling Bodies and discovered the moons of Jupiter; Descartes had introduced coordinates to mathematics. Efforts to understand how nature worked were sporadic and scattered among individuals working alone in various places in Europe. This was the Age of Kings. The Reformation and protracted wars and the Black Death dominated the lives and the attention of the people. The human condition was no different in 1650 than it had been in 300 B.C. when the extent of human knowledge was roughly the same. Human beings had been living, procreating, fighting, and dying for two-thousand years without significant change, yet a mere two-hundred years after 1650, the world of mankind was almost totally changed. What happened? The man standing at that critical juncture in time was identified by Andrew J. Galambos as Isaac Newton.

As I flip a light switch, watch television, drive through town, take my medications, or write on this computer, I think that, without Newton, none of this would exist. Does mankind owe gratitude to Newton? Yes, it does.

Aside from the moral rectitude of gratitude, entrepreneurs and manufacturers have a strong proprietary motive in paying gratitude: attracting the best innovators. The competition for innovators today is fierce and it is often difficult for an innovator to know which company will meet his or her requirements the best; this will quickly help them decide.

In the ever more rapidly changing world that is coming, innovators will seldom deal with a single company for more than a single contract to build a single product and, for the most part, they won't even leave home. All of the old industrial paradigms, including centralized locations, management, interviews, applications, meetings, commuting, paperwork, paydays, and benefits, will be out the window. A contract for a product, with a money-back guarantee, will be all that's necessary. Degrees and endorsements mean nothing in this world, achievement and reputation mean everything. So when an innovator with a good track record goes looking for a new contract, what will he or she look for, besides money? A company which pays gratitude to innovators like himself or herself.

WHO OWNS WHAT: The innovator owns his or her innovation and, therefore, the innovator owns whatever gratitude is deposited into his or her account by the Directory and may designate the use to which it is put. However, we must divide this subject into two categories, dead innovators and living innovators.

Dead innovators cannot instruct the Directory how to use their money. Thus the Directory must unilaterally decide on a use that is implied by the work that innovator accomplished, i.e., an implied contract. Newton, for example, relied on a tree of knowledge that began in ancient times called natural philosophy. He also relied on a tree of knowledge that began in ancient times called alchemy. The Directory distributes gratitude down both trees, but what do they do with the tree of alchemy after Newton? Most likely they would follow the subsequent tree called chemistry.

What does the Directory actually do with the money assigned to dead innovators? By implied contract, the Directory invests it in areas relevant to the innovator. Investments could include companies and mutual funds and could include individuals, i.e., education loans or project loans. Profits from these investments would be reinvested and wealth would accumulate.

Living innovators could have a contract with the Innovation Directory for the use of any gratitude payments. First, a critical distinction must be made: payments made in *gratitude* are not the same thing as payments made for the *use* of an innovation, such as contracted royalties from a corporation; gratitude payments might flood in from thousands of sources for the innovation of one individual while that individual may have only a few contracts with specific entrepreneurs. Since the purpose of the Innovation Directory is justice to innovators, the flow of gratitude payments is one-way. The only contract offered by the Directory to the living innovator concerns investment of money collected in his or her name; it is similar in this respect to trusts, endowments, and scholarships.

INNOVATION REGISTRY: This is a separate service of the Innovation Clearinghouse offered to innovators everywhere who want to have a guaranteed record of their work. The Registry numbers and time and date stamps each entry, which may be totally encrypted by the innovator, for a fee. This verification may be critically important to the innovator at a later date as innovation proliferates at ever increasing volume and speed.

INNOVATION AGENCY: This is a separate service of the Innovation Clearinghouse offered to innovators everywhere who want an agent to handle their contracts and contracted royalties with a money-back guarantee on their service. This service could range from writing specific contracts to investments and insurance. Many innovators simply don't want to be bothered with such things and in the past have left these decisions to non-proprietary institutions who were pleased to steal their innovations while supposedly taking care of their interests.

JUSTICE: Just as positive innovation is rewarded by the Innovation Clearinghouse, negative innovation is punished. This concept could be expanded beyond the creation of and use of the tools of coercion to any act of coercion whatever. This could consist of publication of the individual's name and act plus an assignment of a financial penalty appropriate to the damage inflicted. Whether any actual money is collected is moot. Men like Hitler do not accumulate a positive balance in the Directory to compensate for the negative balance he deserves in Justice, but quantifying the damage will instruct future generations on the man's real worth to mankind.

INSURANCE: There is no reason why any insurance company cannot guarantee the identity of an innovator, but since such insurance does not yet exist, the Innovation Clearinghouse can become the first one to offer it. The integrity of an entry in the Registry is already guaranteed, but an innovator may wish to further protect his or her work by purchasing additional insurance.

ARBITRATION: In the event of a dispute about the identity of an innovator and in the event that one or more of the disputants have no insurance, the Innovation Clearinghouse can offer an arbitration service of equal value to insurance arbitration for a fee with a money-back guarantee of impartial fairness to all parties.

DISCUSSION: My critics have raised questions that I would like to address.

WELFARE: I make no provision for "public welfare" or for "public goods." Harry Browne describes several schemes for privatizing welfare, parks, recreation, and highways in his excellent book, *Why Government Doesn't Work,* and there are many other sources of information on this subject, but what bothers me about this issue is that it is an issue at all. Civilization does not depend on its consumers, civilization depends on its producers. The simple, observable truth is, the "public" does not exist, only individual persons living individual lives exist. My goal is to gradually remove the power of government from the hands of self-serving politicians and bureaucrats and put it into the hands of those same individual persons living individual lives and I see no reason to address the artificial fantasies of political government at all.

MONEY: Since the gratitude paid to innovators belongs to the innovator, why can't he or she write checks against it, borrow against it, or leave it to the kids?

Whereas the traditional self-sustaining trust, endowment, or scholarship is initially funded by an individual, family, or corporation with their own income, in this case the trust is funded by small incremental payments from producers in gratitude to the innovator, not as income paid directly to the innovator by contract. Although the trust exists in the name of the innovator and the use to which it is put may be designated by the innovator, the money itself does not belong to the innovator.

When I sell my literature, for example, I put aside a small percentage of my profits to be paid specifically to my antecedents' accounts when the Innovation Directory exists; I want to pay my gratitude to Andrew J. Galambos, for example, not to his great-grandnephew in Hungary. In a thousand years or in ten-thousand years, the value of my own account in the Innovation Directory will be a measure of my own contribution to the survival of our species and I don't want that degraded by any means. It is my legacy.

Hypothetically, then, money goes into the Innovation Directory and never comes out; what use is that?

Money that goes into the Innovation Directory is invested in real-time industries, research and development, and education for a profit. The only money in use by mankind today is fiat political government money, it's money because they tell us it's money and we take their word for it because we don't have a choice. True wealth, however, resides in innovation, goods, and services, in the production of living individuals. Gradually we can turn that production into real money by investing it in innovation, goods, and services in an institution beyond the reach of political governments; if they can't get their hands on it, they can't destroy it. This wealth will power future generations, not the artificial fantasies of a Federal Reserve Board.

DOMINATION: What is to prevent the Innovation Clearinghouse from becoming an institution of world domination, the very thing you are trying to preclude?

In promoting this paradigm I use the name in the singular to keep my presentation as simple and concise as possible. There is no reason why this kind of business cannot proliferate; the structure is similar to existing directories and search engines and the Registry may even begin in one of them. Thus we can rely in part on competition to keep any one company from dominating the business, let alone dominating the world.

As I have written elsewhere, Andrew J. Galambos said, if you find a risk, insure against it. We don't have that kind of insurance available yet, no more than we have an Innovation Clearinghouse yet, but the one will grow from the other eventually.

But let's say a madman does take over one of these businesses and hands over the latest research on nuclear weapons to the Chinese, like a recent President of the United States did, what do we do then?

First, other businesses can advertise the crime and can refuse to do business with him. Second, innovators can remove all of their registered innovations. Third, insurance companies can demand restitution and apply sanctions and penalties through the network of other clearinghouses and banks. That would be justice.

SUMMARY: An Innovation Clearinghouse will exist to bring justice to innovators, living and dead. It will concomitantly begin to build a stable financial base for future generations. It will operate in concert with institutions of banking and insurance to eliminate the use of coercion in human affairs.

Let us begin.

# Ideological Excerpts from *Atlantis: A Novel about Economic Government*

## 1997

### Anarchy

"Atlantis has powerful enemies, Mr. Conant. Every political state on earth would like to rule or to destroy us. Don't look surprised. Atlantis is the conscious and deliberate antithesis of the political state."

"Do you mean anarchy?"

"No. I mean government, self-government, government by natural law, not by political coercion. It is a concept that my ancestors died for, perhaps your ancestors also. Did any of your family fight in the Revolutionary War?"

"I'm not sure. Why do you ask?"

"They fought for liberty. What they meant by liberty was freedom from government coercion. Unfortunately, the concept had powerful enemies even then. The slave-owning agrarian aristocrats and the slave-trading merchants had everything to lose in the cause for liberty;

the authors of the Constitution were outspoken enemies of liberty. We have such enemies. Come with me."

## Rationality

"Man has no claws," Dupris spoke Siouan, "his jaws and his teeth are weak. Man cannot run like Tatokala the antelope, man cannot fly like Wambli the eagle. Man has not the strength of Mahto the grizzly, nor even the stink of Maka the skunk. Would you not agree, Wahin-Numpa?"

Johnny could not stop shaking. All of his life he had rebuked his friends for not returning to traditional Indian ways, for permitting this "white" Indian to dominate the tribe, yet here he was listening to the language of his people, the language he had never bothered to master. Even his own name sounded strange to him.

"Would you not agree?" Dupris repeated. Johnny appealed to the eyes of his father, but they were as cold as stone.

"Yes. Yes, sir," he said in English.

"Then what are we doing here?" Dupris did not alter his choice of language. "If man is such a puny thing, how did he survive?"

Johnny understood the question but he did not understand the purpose. "Look here," he said, "I know you've caught me. Why don't you just expel me—like the others. I'll go."

The three men were silent, then his father said, "No."

Well, if they did not want to punish him, what did they want?

"Answer my question," Dupris said.

"I don't know the answer."

"Think. How did your ancestors know to kill the Pte? How did they know to cure the meat? How did they survive a million winters without fangs and claws?"

"I don't know. I suppose they had customs, traditions, things like that."

"And where did their customs and traditions originate? Can we find instructions for making a stone axe or a computer chip growing on a tree? Does the wakantanka distribute these instructions in our dreams?"

"Naw, I don't buy that stuff. You know, somebody has an idea or figures out a better way to do things and they try it and that's it."

"Ah. And what do we call this faculty in man?"

"Oh, I get it. Think, you said. Reason."

### Natural Laws of Property

"How do you regulate them?"

"We don't. No business can survive a bad reputation."

"You mean these casino owners can do whatever they want?"

"Within the limits of their contracts with the owner of the building."

Gideon stared unseeing at the dwarf conifers grouped on a mound in the garden. Susie watched the muscles work in his jaw. Clearly he was not pleased. When he looked back at her, his eyes were cold and hostile. "You know that you are giving refuge to gangsters and criminals. You know their money comes from prostitution, drugs, smuggling, and bootlegging. And you control them with contracts?"

"You can buy anything that is for sale," replied Susie mildly, "including sex and drugs, whether it is your so-called legal or not, whether it is here or somewhere else; if people are selling something, other people will buy it if they want it. We're not trying to reconstruct human nature, Gideon, nobody in history has ever been able to do that, we are only providing an environment where it is safe to be human, to live as you wish, to do what you want. The only human activity which is proscribed by contractual agreement is coercion."

"That's impossible! You talk about human nature! There is nothing more fundamental to human nature than force. The strong always win. You've got to have laws, police, courts, jails—to protect the weak and the innocent. You've got to have armies to protect the country. Otherwise you've got anarchy, chaos."

"What have you got out there right now?"

"No. No. You can't use that argument on me. What we need are stronger laws and more jails. The President needs to impose martial law in New York and California."

"Does martial law work in Washington?"

"There hasn't been time." Gideon stopped suddenly, as though he had said too much, yet he had only echoed the strident demands of the media. Susie had heard the same argument all of her life. She sympathized with the intelligent people of the world who had never been exposed to an alternative. It was not easy for men like Gideon to accept the idea that there was an alternative, even when it stared them in the face.

"We do not need police, courts, or jails, Gideon. Our security relies on simple principles that any child can understand and on complex technology that cannot be subverted."

"What principles?"

"That sentient beings live to pursue happiness. That any definition of happiness is valid that does not include coercion. That every individual has a natural right to his life, to his innovations, and to his wealth."

Gideon stared at the garden for several minutes. "Any technology can be subverted."

Like many others, Gideon appeared to allow the disclosure of Atlantis' real foundation slide past without notice. Susie was disappointed. The technology was of minor importance.

"Not ours," Susie stated, "I guarantee it."

"Did you build it?"

"No. It built itself, you might say. Certainly we designed and installed the hardware and the software, but after a point the software takes care of itself."

"Somebody could rearrange the original configuration, change the rules."

"Somebody could have done so in the beginning. It's too late now."

"Really? What if somebody tried?"

"Somebody would find themselves on a plane bound for elsewhere."

"So that's how it works?"

"Yes, that's how it works."

Susie wondered at the twist that their conversation had taken. She wondered if Gideon was expressing simple curiosity or something else. Merchants were generally satisfied to know that they were safe from criminal predation; she could not recall any who doubted it after their first day in the city.

"You included innovation as property," Gideon continued, "I have two questions. Why? And how can you keep track of such nebulous property?"

He had listened! Susie revised her earlier judgment and qualified her suspicions. "Your knowledge and comprehension of ideas belongs to you as surely as your brain belongs to you. If you extrapolate from existing ideas and invent a new idea, that innovation belongs to you. You owe gratitude to the discoverers of the existing ideas that you started with. If subsequent innovators use your idea, they owe gratitude to you. The question becomes why do we owe gratitude? Because innovation is property, ideas are property, and when you use somebody else's property to earn money, you owe them for it. Keeping track of who owns what is easy with computers."

"Sounds a little wacky to me. What does it get you?"

"Atlantis is what it gets you, a whole lot of very selfish, creative, productive people who have very selfish, proprietary notions about who controls their innovations, themselves, or some failed haberdasher from Missouri."

Gideon looked a little wide-eyed at her angry sarcasm. "I don't understand the reference."

"Truman," Susie spat the name like a curse, "President Harry S. Truman, the man who ordered the use of atomic energy to slaughter innocent people."

"But Susie, that was long ago."

"And nothing has changed out there. You still have two-bit crooks telling the men and women of genius what to do, then stealing their innovations and turning them into evil machines of coercion."

Susie looked away. The depth of her anger toward injustice often embarrassed her, but she refused to compromise her judgment. She could feel Gideon's eyes on her and she looked back at him. He smiled faintly. What was it? Agreement? Approval? Mockery? She couldn't tell.

Gideon changed the subject. "Back there in the car you said that many doctors come here but that few stay. Why is that?"

"They are attracted by the promise of independence, but when they learn about the risk they usually leave."

"What risk?"

"I guarantee my work, Gideon. If a customer is not satisfied, I don't get paid. If I make a mistake that results in damage or harm, my insurance company pays for it and my premium goes up."

Gideon chuckled. "I'd like to see one of these National Health Service doctors swallow that pill."

"It isn't a pleasant sight. They usually threaten us with Washington, but then everybody who gets caught in their own contradictions does that."

"How do you manage to keep the government out of here."

"We don't. That is to say, there is no entity in Atlantis who seeks to keep anybody out. They have no jurisdiction here, their laws do not apply here, and they have no means of exercising their coercive powers here."

Gideon frowned as if in deep concentration. Susie waited. She watched his muscled hand toy with the delicate china cup. He looked up.

"What do you mean by coercion?"

"Any interference with the property of another."

"Taxation."

"Yes."

"Tariffs, regulation of commerce."

"Yes."

"You fly into the face of the Constitution, you break the fundamental law of the land."

"The Constitution was written by slave-owning planters and slave-trading merchants…"

"That's not true."

"…who wanted an armed central government to protect their own interests…"

"That's not true, either."

"…and who had no premonition of the coming revolution."

"What revolution?"

"The Industrial Revolution."

### Insurance

Then there were the insurance companies. He could insure anything from his life to his cufflinks and the policies and the rates were posted right there in the directory with no fine print. Life insurance policies ran into the millions with the lowest rates he'd ever seen. That could only mean that they thought there was little risk. There was innovation insurance and investment insurance and contract insurance and marriage insurance and health insurance that was complete and cheap; there was even murder insurance in case you lost your mind and killed somebody. Every single insurance company advertised a money-back guarantee.

## Constitution

"I'll remember to be careful, Mahtowin." Gideon smiled, held her chair once again, and sat down opposite. "I wanted to ask you," he continued, "what you've got against the Constitution?"

The audacity! Susie glared at him. "Article One, Section Eight, do you want me to recite it for you?"

Gideon shrugged. "I'm reasonably familiar. It authorized Congress..."

"Tyrannical powers."

"Which are restrained by the executive and the judicial branches."

Susie quit huffing. Evidently the man's curiosity was sincere, but why should he invite her to such a place to discuss politics?

"Gideon, there are history and government programs on the public net."

"I haven't had time. Besides, I want to hear you tell me."

Maybe so. "I can tell you that it is very simple. When they separated church and state, they should have separated commerce and state too. The one concept is no more radical than the other. But they couldn't, not without changing the status-quo of slavery. They would have lost support from both the slave states and the shipping states. They wouldn't have had much of a convention."

"You imply that slavery was the main issue."

"It was then, it was a century earlier, and it continued to be a century later."

"But it was Hamilton who instigated things. He didn't own slaves."

"He didn't need to, he married money, New York merchant money. Hamilton was disappointed with the Constitution. He wanted a President for life who held absolute power. He wanted an American king and an aristocracy and a whole country of slaves. All of those men were trying to institutionalize a contradiction. The Constitution begins, 'We the people of the United States.' But, to them, Indians, Negroes, and women were not people. Women and slaves were property, like cattle, and Indians belonged to another species, like dogs and rats."

"I think you are exaggerating the case."

"Not at all. When people persist in trying to maintain a contradiction they must resort to force. Look at the historical facts. You can't turn a blind eye to the humanness and equality of women, Negroes, and Indians without force. This master and slave mentality has been a part of political government since Sumer and Akkad in ancient Babylonia. It was the invention and application of machines that could do the work of a civilization that rendered slavery obsolete. The authors of the Constitution had no idea that such machines were coming in the very next generation and they had no reason to believe in anything except the status quo."

Susie knew she was going too fast, pushing the boundaries too vigorously, but the man had asked for it. She could not read his face. He appeared intent and alert with none of the anger he had expressed before.

"What about Washington? Was he going to become Hamilton's king?"

"If Hamilton could have had his way. I see Washington as the middle man, as the arbiter of differences. He had more in common with the uneducated farmers and frontiersmen than he had with the genteel Jefferson. He had embraced the principles of liberty created by Thomas Paine, but once Paine went to France his opinion swung back. He also married money, but his came with slaves. I've often wondered if the slave clause was his idea."

"I'm sorry, you've lost me."

"Article One, Section Nine begins by restricting Congress from passing laws that would control the importation of slaves for the next twenty years. Washington was fifty-five at the time. I wonder if that clause was his compromise with the other Virginia planters."

"You mean that he wouldn't have to address the problem in his own lifetime?"

"Yes, there's that, but the clause also gave the planters twenty years to get out of the business."

"I suppose it also gave the abolitionists some reason to support the ratification."

"Possibly."

Susie watched Gideon carefully push bits of his expensive gourmet dinner around his plate, as though he would discover some vital truth in the rearrangement. Why is this discussion so important to him?

"I would have thought that the power to tax would be your major objection to the Constitution."

"The colonies were heavily in debt after the Revolution and the Articles of Confederation promised to pay that debt. The people who benefited from their newfound liberty should have paid for it, but most of them were bankrupt themselves—Shay's Rebellion was literally a debtor's revolt. I think taxation was inevitable."

"But you say taxation is an unnecessary evil."

"We are living two centuries later. If they had separated commerce and state, however, they would have discovered that principle sooner."

Gideon quit playing with his food and leaned back in his chair. "You know, Susie, I'd like to believe you, but when you take the state out of commerce all I can see is chaos. I see drug companies selling poison, car companies selling lemons, foreign companies selling cheap. I see people out of work and rioting in the streets. I see the end of America."

Susie heard the plea in his voice, a plea to verify or renounce, like a patient asking his doctor for the bitter truth. "I could answer you as I did before and ask what have you got out there right now, but I won't. The one thing that the state has that no individual has is the threat of and the use of unlimited physical force. If the state wants to impose wage and price controls, establish import and export quotas, regulate communication and transportation systems, it can do so only because it has a monopoly on coercion. Eliminate coercion, however, and the state becomes irrelevant. Commerce, by itself, cannot force anybody to buy anything."

"And the Constitution? Could they have eliminated coercion?"

"Of course not, Gideon, the Constitution is the enabling instrument of coercion. If they had separated commerce and state, however, they could have devoted their coercive power solely to matters of justice."

"But it was the commercial interests that asked the state to intervene on their behalf."

"Precisely, Gideon. Religions also asked the state to intervene on their behalf and the state declined. What if the state told the commercial interests the same thing? That intervention was unconstitutional?"

Gideon leaned forward. "Look, Susie, every industrialized state uses its resources to help its businesses compete in world markets."

"Which is one reason they move their research and development departments here."

"Why is that?"

"Security. No state military-industrial espionage department can spy on them here. They can't steal from each other and they can't sabotage each other. In fact, we give them some very good reasons not to try. We provide that 'level playing field' that political conservatives like to promise and can't deliver."

### Lifeboat Cases

"I see. So the criminal is trapped by the transportation system, right? He has nowhere to go. But he could hang around here, couldn't he?"

"He could, but the facilities won't work for him, not even the toilets."

"So he puts the stone back or he buys it."

"If the dealer wants to sell it to him."

"Why wouldn't he?"

"Nobody wants to deal with a thief, Jake."

"Then what happens to him?"

"He will soon find himself at the airport. If he pays the restitution posted by the victim's insurance company, he is allowed back into the city, with a certain reputation tacked to his name. Stealing is a losing proposition in Atlantis."

Jake turned it over in his mind for a minute. "What about a child?" He thought he had found a hitch in their system.

"The merchants own their goods and lease their space and they are free to deal with anybody they wish. What you really want to know is whether the city would eject a child and the answer is yes. A child has the same rights and the same responsibilities as an adult. Presumably the child would have insurance too, he would have the same restitution and reputation problems to cope with."

"Where are the parents in this?"

"Wherever they want to be. Children do not belong to their parents, human beings cannot be owned, so parents may be involved in the negotiations if they and their child wish or they may not, if they wish, or the child wishes."

This concept of justice was ruthless, inhuman by the standards Jake grew up with, yet it informed you of exactly where you stood with sparking clarity. He looked up again. It was like the law of gravity, a solemn, silent, force that applied equally, impersonally, and blindly to everybody. That's the way justice should be.

"I don't mean to be difficult, Sarah, but what do you do with birth defects?"

"That's all right, Jake, answering tough questions is part of my job. You must understand, there is no entity that does anything about anything not related to security and the computer programs take care of that. There is no ruler, there are no autocrats or bureaucrats, nobody who makes up rules that affect other people's property. Now, the first property right in nature is the right to your own life. If some other person or government claims the right to your life by force, then you can have no rights at all, zero, you are a slave. Corollary to that is the right to your own body. A child within a woman's body has no rights because it is still a physical part of her body. A laboratory can tell a woman if the fetus is normal in the first trimester, quick, easy, and cheap. Finally, insurance is available to cover the risk. If a woman could be found here so irrational as to ignore prenatal testing and to refuse to buy insurance, well, her problem is one the people who live in Atlantis did not create and will not solve. If the child somehow survives and grows up incapable of comprehending the natural laws of property, the city may finally have to eject it. That would be the ultimate lifeboat case."

"I beg your pardon?"

"The lifeboat case is the argument always used by political government to separate an individual from his money. Generically, it goes like this. There are two men in a lifeboat, one has no arms and the other has no legs, both are deaf, dumb, and blind; what are we going to do about these poor men? Humans are, by and large, gregarious and kind-hearted and can be persuaded to stop everything they are doing and run to their rescue. On an international scale, that translates into wholesale robbery of the many for the sake of the few, with a large percentage of the take going to the robbers themselves, of course, for administrative purposes. You can put anybody into the lifeboat and make the argument work. The starving children of Whatsupland need food. The fact that they are being deliberately starved by their own government is never mentioned. Nobody is supposed to question a lifeboat case. Why are they in the lifeboat? Why are they my responsibility? In Atlantis, the lifeboat sinks. An incompetent person cannot survive here, period, and we are not going to dismantle the city and return to the egalitarian Dark Ages to save him. However, only in Atlantis can you buy insurance to cover the risk and thus avoid becoming a lifeboat case in the first place."

## Innovation Clearing House 1

"He didn't tell you about the Innovation Clearing House?"

"No. It sounds like a federal bureaucracy."

"It's hardly that. In fact, it's the heart of the city, it's the reason the city is able to exist. Did Mr. Dupris tell you how long his lease runs?"

"Yes, a thousand years," Jake shook his head, "it's incredible. It's hard to believe the Sioux Nation took him seriously."

"Not really. Many of the Sioux subscribe to traditions that go back several thousand years. You see, Mr. Dupris expanded the concept of paying honor and respect to those ancestors who enhanced our survival to paying them, period."

"What? That's outrageous! You can't pay dead people. What for?"

"Ideas, Jake," Sarah said calmly, watching him fume.

"Ideas! Preposterous! Everybody knows you can't own ideas. Ideas are public domain. And you certainly can't pay dead people for their ideas. How on earth could you? Oh, I get it, that's what this Clearing House is all about, isn't it? Well, it's crazy."

Jake couldn't say why this concept troubled him so much. He felt attracted to this woman, he liked her looks, he liked her voice, and he liked her thinking, until now. It was as though a beautiful child suddenly started cursing. He felt betrayed by an unexpected obstacle to his attraction. Then he noticed that she was watching him, judging his reaction, and he became even more uncomfortable. Maybe coming here had been a mistake after all.

"If it's any consolation," Sarah said, "almost everybody thinks its crazy the first time they hear it. Some even pack up and leave for a while. Every first-time visitor to Atlantis gets a custom tour and gets an introduction to the natural laws of property. It's too much for some, I hope it's not too much for you."

### Innovation Clearing House 2

"I'm so happy for you, Jake," she had said most sincerely. "Is the mill going to be a new application of laser technology?"

"Far as I know," he had answered. "The physics and engineering people never heard of it, that's for sure."

"Then that makes it a new innovation."

"Yeah, now you mention it, I reckon it is. I never thought of it that way before."

"And it's your own idea."

"Sure it is. But I could never put it together myself. They're going to have to show me how to turn the thing on."

"And you are paying them to build it and show you how it works?"

"You bet. Say, what are you driving at?"

"Will you get paid by future generations who use your innovation?"

"I don't know. What do you mean? You think I should patent it?"

"Would you pay the men who invented the laser, Jake?"

The question had stopped him. If he was going to earn money using their innovation, then he should pay them for it. And if somebody was going to earn money with his innovation, then he should get paid for it. What was so hard about that?

"Innovation Clearing House, you're talking about those idea accounts, aren't you?"

"Yes, Jake."

"Because it's not right to build with stolen tools."

"Yes, Jake."

"I think I need to talk to those people."

"Yes, Jake."

He thought about it for a moment. "What's it going to cost me, Sarah?"

"One-tenth of one-percent of your profits."

He had had to laugh then and the memory brought a chuckle to him now. Pennies, that's all it amounted to. But later he added it up. If this thing did go on and on, as Dupris said it would, those accounts would grow into billions, billions loaned out for research, education, development, loaned to people like himself, people with investment potential. He would earmark his own account for timber farming.

## Foundation of Wealth

As their celebration drew to a close, Peter Dupris arose once more and addressed the gathering.

"Thanks to you, Atlantis has survived this latest assault by the political state. Now we must remain alert for further attacks. The next few years will be critical. As our sister cities are completed and more and more of the innovators and the entrepreneurs of our planet come to live and to work with us, the state will become ever more desperate to stop us. Political coercion cannot compete with freedom, it can only try to destroy it. However, let us not forget that the future of the political state is of no meaningful concern to the real purpose of Atlantis. I do not care what happens to the political state, I only want to be left alone.

"I built this city to protect individual man's life, innovations, and wealth. I built this city to bring absolute justice to human relationships. Here, men and women of integrity and self-esteem can be confident of their freedom to live as they choose. After life itself, it is the freedom of innovation which we exist to protect.

"Until man develops a rational relationship with innovation, innovation will always threaten to destroy him. The individuals who developed atomic energy should be rewarded for their innovations, then punished for relinquishing control of their innovations to the political state. In Atlantis, these values, both positive and negative, are assessed, recorded, and compensated.

"Innovation may proceed slowly or quickly, it may arise in isolation or in a dozen places at once, but it is always the result of an individual mind working alone to solve some problem. That individual may have a thousand antecedents and a thousand successors; all are compensated. This is not only simple justice to our predecessors and justice to our peers, it is also a rational incentive for generations to come. When innovators of the future can depend on growing gratitudes for centuries after they are gone, they can control the use of their innovations and prevent their theft or misuse by future generations.

"The very concept of wealth itself is tied to innovation as private property. Thus the value of wealth is fixed to something more permanent than gold, more permanent than this planet, more permanent than this galaxy. With innovation as the standard, Homo Sapiens can become a truly stellar species. This destiny Atlantis exists to guarantee."

(Note from the author: A proprietary city on land, a ship at sea, or a space vehicle in space is founded on free, non-coercive, contractual relationships. For an example of such a contract, see Spencer MacCallum's prototype at <http://www.freenation.org/fnf/a/f33m1.html>.)

# Bridge to A Free Nation

## 1999

A free nation is an ideal that has been on my mind since 1965, when I attended meetings of a group who intended to create one. The results were disappointing. During the 1970s I studied under Andrew J. Galambos at his Free Enterprise Institute and there learned some of the mechanisms for providing security and justice without a coercive state, but the free nation in which these might be applied eluded all of us. Perhaps out of frustration with the improbability of this dream, I spent many years writing a novel about it. Today, thanks to the Internet, I believe we may be closer than ever before to creating a free nation and I believe it may be much closer to home than we imagine. Let me explain.

The model of government which I most admire was described by Spencer MacCallum in *Formulations* (Vol. VI, No. 3); it is a fine extrapolation of the multiple-tenant income property from shopping malls and cruise ships to a mercantile city in which native citizens are economic partners in the venture. This makes sense to me. His proposed method of supplying security and justice within the community via the initial lease contract, insurance, and private arbitration (*Formulations*, Vol. III, No. 3) also makes sense to me. I wonder if these concepts might have a broader, more general application in our world today in existing cities and other political jurisdictions? I think it may be possible.

Based on what I learned from Galambos, I put together a simple model which I called economic government (*Formulations*, Vol. VI, No. 1), which consists of intermeshed businesses of insurance, banking, and innovation. Without going into the primary functions of these businesses, a coincidental function could be to provide security and justice within a population, similar to what Mr. MacCallum proposed. The question before us is, how do we get from here to there, how do we make the models work?

One elemental problem which faces every taxpayer on Earth is, how can I keep more of my own money? One answer is to turn it into gold and then hide it, but hidden gold cannot grow, so that's a poor answer. Another answer is to hide it in a numbered account in an offshore investment bank, but that takes a lot of money and a lot of faith in the political jurisdiction where the bank is located, where they know who you are. What if we could hide our after-tax disposable income in small increments in an investment bank in cyberspace where all transactions are encrypted and anonymous and guaranteed? Over time there might be a vast repository of growing wealth owned by ordinary people and hidden from all political governments. Soon all of our financial business could be conducted in cyberspace using anonymous digital cash.

Another elemental problem which faces all of us is the protection of our property, I mean our lives, our physical property, and our intellectual property; it is abundantly clear that the state is intent on stealing our property, not protecting it. One method of protection is insurance, although insurance as we know it today is just another strong arm of the state. But what if we could go on-line and buy insurance cheaply for any risk we can imagine? What if that insurance company had a proprietary interest in reducing its losses by reducing our risk? Freed from the fetters of the state, insurance in cyberspace could become a friendly partner in planning the protection of our property.

What keeps banking and insurance honest? Competition, reputation, and a plain money-back-guarantee to do what they say they will do. How long would a business survive a bad reputation in cyberspace? Maybe one day, maybe two. A company that can't live up to its guarantees will also vanish in a short time. The free-market in cyberspace will ensure that we have dependable, trustworthy, guaranteed banking, investment, and insurance available to all of us.

I think the bridge to a free nation exists in cyberspace and I think we are already on it. Anonymous digital cash is urgently needed by the international business community and that demand will soon be filled. Investment banking in cyberspace is a reality and only a little nudging will convince them to sever their bonds with the state. Strong encryption exists, free to any person. If the state tries to throttle the Internet via the service providers, which is happening in Britain and Australia, they can move their servers outside of the throttling jurisdiction; an ISP can serve the world as well from a Pacific atoll as it can from London or Sydney. But if the bridge exists in cyberspace, where does it go?

I was discussing these prospects with a friend the other day and I happened to quip, "The next time San Francisco goes bankrupt, let's buy it." And the models began to fall into place.

The collapse of political governments is well documented in history; the uncertain questions for us are when and how fast. Being an optimist by nature, I will assume a best case situation where the failure begins on a municipal level and gradually spreads. Operating in the safety of cyberspace, a corporation might be formed along the lines envisioned by Mr. MacCallum to buy the land in the afflicted region in partnership with the citizens and restore the region to its former prosperity as a multiple-tenant income property. Taking into account the investment potential of unfettered wealth in cyberspace, we might discover that the free nation we seek may not be too far from home after all.

(Originally published in *formulations*, A Publication of the Free Nation Foundation, Vol. VII, No. 1, Autumn 1999. See <http://www.freenation.org>.)

# Government Malpractice

## 1993–2000

Government practices medicine without a license. The Constitution does not license government to practice medicine. Government practices medicine by paying for, or by refusing to pay for, medical goods and services; by approving, or not approving, medications, treatment devices, machines, and medical procedures; and by paying for, or by blocking, medical research. In short, as long as government controls the purse strings, government controls medicine. But the money belongs to us. Government has no money it did not steal.

Gross Domestic Product (GDP) is a measure of wealth created in this country. Health care costs are projected at 14% of GDP (1993). So what? If I want to spend 25% of my own personal income on health care and push up the % GDP a fraction, so what? But if you want to spend even one cent of my personal income on your health care, or on your swimming pool, or on anything you care to buy with my money, you will find me fighting you for all I am worth, fighting for my life. Mr. Clinton wants my money, my life, to benefit you, your life; Mr. Clinton wants your money, your life, to benefit me, my life. I don't need Mr. Clinton to make decisions for me, thank you, and neither do you. We can make our own decisions. Mr. Clinton has promised, however, against my wishes and without my sanction, to limit health care spending. Without going to the wall over ideology just yet, I ask one simple question: Has your government ever limited any spending?

In 1991 President Bush promised to reduce government debt in exchange for higher taxes. He got the taxes, we got the debt. In 1993 President Clinton promised the exactly the same thing using the same words. He got the taxes. Government debt is expected to increase from 55% GDP to 65% GDP by 2004. This is not encouraging.

Let's look at congressional benefits: $353 Million in 1970, $2.7 Billion in 1992. Those girls and boys in congress really do know who comes first: They do. Is this an example of spending restraint?

Federal entitlement programs include Social Security, Medicare, Medicaid, food stamps, unemployment, veteran benefits, farm aid, and federal employee benefits. These are all unfunded contingent liabilities, that is to say, the money is taken from your pocket and put into their pocket. No, madam, there is no reserve account with your name on it earning interest somewhere. Entitlements are strictly hand-to-mouth. This year (1993) entitlement programs will cost us $1 Trillion, more than the entire federal budget in 1981 ($696 Billion). Do you really believe government can contain costs?

When Medicare went into effect on July 1, 1965, government practice of medicine was fairly benign. Medical goods were supplied and services were rendered, bills were sent off to regional third-party payers, that is, to private insurance companies contracted by Medicare to process the paperwork, and the bills were usually paid. This system was called "fee-for service", a familiar economic concept at the time, like the idea of paying for what you get. However, since the "government" was paying for it, the demand for services suddenly escalated.

Also in the early days of Medicare, there was another influence at work. It was called the Hill-Burton Act. After 1965 hospitals were overwhelmed with business, they needed to expand, they needed huge capital investment. Government rushed in to guarantee loans and to provide money for new construction and new equipment. Hospitals that had functioned well for years, for decades in some cases, were encouraged by government to take the plunge into long-term capital debt.

Almost overnight, medicine in this country became an expensive proposition. Mr. Clinton says his program is going to limit prices. Somebody should tell him that Medicare has been trying to do precisely that for the last quarter-century. Medicare administrators attempted to control expenses by establishing a uniform set of prices (called price fixing) for goods and services; everything from facial tissues to brain surgery was assigned a price. Hospitals could charge whatever price they wished, of course, this wasn't socialized medicine! But Medicare would only pay part of the price they approved. On a bill for one-thousand dollars, say, Medicare might approve only five-hundred, then pay eighty-percent of that. Currently, hospitals anticipate getting back about thirty-percent of billing to Medicare-Medicaid—that's thirty cents on the dollar. This is one way government limits prices..

Often the hospital doesn't get paid at all. When the allotted tax revenues run low, the Medicare third-party payers invent forms demanding justification of charges. This tactic proved so successful at delaying payment or denying payment altogether that it quickly became the standard of the insurance industry.

Then there was outright theft. Years after medical goods and services had been rendered and paid, Medicare could decide to retroactively revoke payment. Five years might pass before Medicare announced to a hospital that they were taking back two-million dollars in "overpayments" made five years ago.

In the face of declining "fees" for increased "services", health-care providers raised their prices. Please note that it was your government that promoted the service and then, by refusing to pay for it, forced prices to rise. The clamor to curb health-care costs went on the political agenda in the Reagan era. His administration's Medicare Reform Act attacked the problem at its source: Medical bills. And they found the perfect solution: Don't pay them. The half measures listed above remained in place but were, at best, haphazard, and the third-party payers were constrained by the fee-for-service provision in the old law. That provision was eliminated. It was replaced by Diagnostic Related Groups, DRGs. Now hospitals get paid, if and when they get paid, for the diagnosis regardless of the expense incurred. Thus, if a patient responds to treatment in the time specified by some bureaucrat for his or her diagnosis, the hospital may break even, but if the patient doesn't respond in the time specified, the hospital loses whatever the treatment costs. The hospital, of course, has fixed expenses like that huge capital debt incurred in the good old days and the wages and benefits of employees. Thus for every patient who will not get well in the prescribed time, usually the elderly and the chronically ill, the hospital loses money, a lot of money. For example, a patient with chronic lung disease on life support machines can generate more lost revenue in a week than a typical R.N. earns in a year. Hospitals are real businesses, their books have to balance somehow, and if they do not have the income to pay employees, capital debt, venders, and suppliers, then either they go out of business or they cut back services. America has lost over three hundred hospitals to bankruptcy since the passage of the Medicare Reform Act and hundreds more are closing beds and laying off nurses as you read this. At the rate we're going, by the time every man, woman, and child in the country gets his Medicare card in the mail, the hospitals will be dark, boarded-up, vacant buildings. But we will all have equal access (to nothing) and health-care spending will finally be under control.

The worst attacks by the politicians and by the media in the pitch for health care reform have been suffered by the medical doctors. Doctors are the most visible people in the business, doctors are held responsible for everything that happens in the business, and doctors are the smallest minority of health-care providers in the business. Doctors make good targets. Doctors have been treated even worse than hospitals by government. Not only has Medicare fixed the fees that they can charge, it has rolled them back! Hospital employees negotiate income raises every couple of years; doctors take income cuts every couple of years. That many doctors are quietly disappearing from the health-care scene is only coincidental.

For the sake of argument let's assume the government can keep a health-care system of sorts running by nationalizing the hospitals and drafting the doctors, nurses, and technicians into the army to keep them from quitting, a tactic that has more or less worked elsewhere on this planet, there is still one problem: Money. Where is the money coming from to pay for this grand expansion of socialism? The system will only work if the number of tax-payers grows faster than the number of tax-receivers. Both the governments of England and of Sweden have recently announced cutbacks in health-care services and increases in out-of-pocket expenses for the services that are left. They say that they are running out of tax-payers. Service goes down, price goes up, that's how socialized medicine works. The American middle class is not growing. American business is not growing. In short, the number of tax-payers is not growing. The only thing that's growing in this country is debt, inflation, unemployment, and welfare. The number of tax-receivers is growing. When everybody becomes a tax-receiver, where is the money coming from? Remember, government has no money it does not steal.

Your government is good at collecting taxes from honest people, so beware: They are thinking about stealing your "tax expenditures". This bizarre concept refers to taxes which could be, but never have been, levied against you. Let's look at some of them. Employer-paid health insurance could be taxed for about $75 Billion. Home mortgage interest could be taxed for $46 Billion. All income and benefits for personal income greater than $200,000.00 could be taxed for $5 Billion. The $372 Billion in federal benefits that go to those people who earn between $30,000.00 and $200,000.00 a year could be eliminated or taxed. Do you really believe that your elected representatives in congress, the very people who gave themselves a 700% increase in benefits over the last twenty years, are going to continue to ignore these sources of tax revenue? But, don't worry, there will never be enough money to pay for socialized medicine in this country.

When the American government completes the socialization of medicine in this country, here's how it will work. Pneumonia will have to go home in three days, period, cured or not. Fractured hip will have to stay home (and catch pneumonia) until they can fit it into the abbreviated surgery schedule. Lacerated arm will get five stitches instead of twenty-five. Grandma will have to live with her bunions. Grandpa will have to live with his hernia. Sunday morning chest pain will have to wait for the clinic to open on Monday, then wait six hours for an EKG to confirm she had a heart attack. Intensive care units, cardiac units, and emergency rooms will be closed down and exotic surgery, like open heart surgery, will not be done. Ethical questions about genetic research, miracle drugs, and pulling the plug will need no further discussion, there will be no research, no drugs, and no plug. More and more doctors will retire with mysterious ailments, to be replaced by nurses, nurses' aides and barbers in public clinics that will be open Monday through Friday, 9 to 5 , call for an appointment.

What can be done about the health care "crisis" that your government has created.? First, government must get out of the health care business. Poison does not cure poisoning. Second, private insurance companies and private hospitals have to wake up to the realities of socialism and to the potential of a free market health-care industry.

The first proposition will occur no matter what else happens. Government has no money it does not steal and the victims of this crime grow fewer every day. If your government does nothing but stand pat, the health care system will fail. If government does something, anything but admit to its malpractice and quit, the system will fail.

The second proposition does not seem likely but it is our only chance. Private insurance companies and private hospitals could, if they wished, and if political government would leave them alone, begin to drag the system backwards out of the hands of government bureaucrats and politicians. Rolling back bureaucracy would be an unprecedented historical event! There are many obstacles, of course, not the least of which is that many government bureaucrats and health-care bureaucrats and insurance company bureaucrats are one and the same people. But it is not impossible, like falling up is impossible. Insurance companies, unlike government, own things that produce wealth; they don't simply steal or print money. They own real estate which is rented or leased, they own businesses which manufacture and distribute goods and services, they own stocks and corporate bonds which pay dividends and interest. Private, profit seeking hospitals are not in such good shape but they are not yet extinct either. Combined, these financial entities could muster enough wealth to do the job. What they lack is the inspiration and the power. This can only come from us, the tax-payers and the consumers. We have to create the market demand for a return to free-market health-care.

Let me contrast a free-market system to the government system with an hypothetical example. Suppose I have suffered an illness which costs fifty-thousand dollars to treat and suppose I have paid only one-thousand dollars into either system. Where does the extra forty-nine thousand dollars come from? In the government system, it comes from taxes, period. Government has no money it does not steal. In the free market system, it comes from profit earning investments made by the insurance company, from wealth that is created, not stolen.

There is an unfulfilled market already for cash and carry health-care delivery and some group of providers, doctors, nurses, technicians, and entrepreneurs could develop it. Take away the vast bureaucracies and the mountains of paperwork, take away the billions of dollars in unpaid bills, and it would cost you ten dollars to see your doctor, not sixty, and your doctor would make a profit. You'd be able to get that rotten appendix out for the price of a new set of tires. Cash only, major credit cards accepted. Ask for it.

Sooner or later your government will get out of the health-care delivery business; either now, while the business is alive; or later, after the business is dead. Tell your politicians and the government bureaucrats to get out of the health care business now and tell your doctors, your hospitals, and your insurance companies to free themselves from government control. You will have affordable, comprehensive health-care delivery in America whenever you, the taxpayer, put a stop to government malpractice.

Update 1997.1: In the unanticipated economic boom wrought by what Simon Buckingham calls technological capitalism, the politicians heave a sigh of relief and tell us that the national debt will be gone in five years and that we are home free. They even cut income taxes. Let's not talk about relentless increases in Social Security and Medicare deductions from our paychecks, they're not taxes, and let's not talk about the government bond debt that our children get to pay. And in the world of health-care we have giant corporations buying bankrupt little hospitals, doctors selling private practices to large groups who can protect their interests, and HMOs. An improvement, you say? Let's look at it.

I call this phenomenon privatized socialism, though in reality it should be called by that old fashioned, unpopular word, fascism, a system where the means of production is privately owned, but the control of production lies in government regulation, e.g., you own the land, but government tells you what you can do with it. Watch where your money goes. It goes from your pocket to and through a bureaucracy, public or private, to a service provider who gives you the wheelchair, the medication, or the surgery. What's wrong with that? You get sick and you go to a doctor. No. First you call your HMO and get their permission and they tell you which doctor you may visit. That doctor says you need to see a specialist. Your HMO says no. Your doctor wants to run some tests. Your HMO says no. Who is this HMO practicing medicine? It's some minimally educated person sitting at a computer terminal in some other state running your doctor's request through a simple algorithm matching symptoms with tests and treatments. So what if she's having a bad day and hits the wrong key? You decide to go the Emergency Room. Fine, but your HMO won't pay for it. You decide to see another doctor. Can't. His group is contracted to see only those patients enrolled in another HMO.

Medicare does it a little differently; they let you go to an approved provider, get treated, then refuse to pay the provider. What do the politicians tell us? They will curtail Medicare spending by further limiting payments to providers. What does this mean? It means that providers are going to change what it is they provide.

Enter the corporations. The idea is, if they can scatter the losses among a sufficient number of hospitals with access to a large enough population, they can still make money. How do you sell something at a loss and still make money? You alter what it is you are selling.

The changes inside the health-care industry have been sudden and devastating. It's all about money now and with revenues declining, the only way to make money is to cut costs; the only way to cut costs is to cut service. The only problem remaining is how to cut service without getting caught in the maze of rules and regulations that surrounds the industry? Watch and see.

The hot-button word in Medicare today is FRAUD. What is Medicare fraud? AARP would like us to believe that it is a monstrous collusion among health-care providers to bilk the taxpayers out of billions of dollars. No, it's more like this. The latest Medicare reform simply denies payment for services for some diagnosis. Example: Medicare will not pay for pre-operative screening tests, like EKGs. So your doctor sends you to the hospital for a pre-op EKG. The hospital has three choices. One, refuse the service. Well, they can't do that, it's against the law. Two, provide the service for free. Possible, but for how long? What happens in the long run? Three, change the billing code from pre-op to cardiomyopathy. There is your fraud. Providers everywhere have responded to the new Medicare regulations by changing billing codes so that they can get paid a little and remain in business. Does this resemble anything you've heard of before?

The end result is going to be the same as I predicted four years ago, but Clinton Socialism won't get the blame, which is a shame. Every doctor I know is planning an early retirement, some are already gone. A brave and hearty few have opened cash-only practices, almost a black-market kind of operation. Health-care bureaucracies continue to grow while health-care providers decline. In the end, when the money runs out, I predict a cut-and-run stampede from both the HMOs and the corporations, much like the Savings and Loan disaster, for much the same reasons, leaving the consumer with no health-care industry at all—private enterprise takes the hit and government takes over and no one will mention the legislation that made it all happen.

The window of opportunity that I thought I saw in 1993 has shut. Nothing short of total deregulation and total withdrawal of government interference can save this industry now.

So who am I to say? I have been employed as a professional care-giver in hospitals since 1963, before Medicare began. I watched it happen.

Update 1997.2: Congress got busy this year and expanded the HMO concept to new depths, authorizing the creation of PPOs, POSs, PSOs, and MSAs. Please note that these "private" programs do not pop into existence because the market demands them, they pop into existence because congress creates them. And just why is congress creating so many alternatives to Medicare? Because Medicare, through its third-party payers, the insurance companies, has been unable curtail spending even through the draconian limitations imposed in earlier legislation and because people are wising up about who is to blame for reduced services and complex claims procedures. These voluntary, for a while, alternatives to Medicare are mandated to micro-manage health-care services on a patient by patient basis and they are baited with financial incentives to do a good job of it. Even AARP, the premier advocate of socialism in America, is issuing dire warnings to its membership to watch out for fraud and abuse from these new programs. The question is, again, who is doing the micro-managing? Not your doctor, you can bet on that. Any doctor? Somewhere? On paper, maybe, but in reality it will be that semi-educated high-school graduate sitting at a computer terminal running your requests through a simple algorithm and giving you a yes/no based on the results. So what if he/she clicks the wrong box, he/she goes home at five anyway.

Accountability: Congress definitely does not want to get stuck holding this bag when it perforates, now predicted to happen in 2010. They have a decade to shift the blame into this new "private" sector that they have created and they made great strides in this direction in 1997. And when the bag breaks, every congressperson in this great land can stand up and point righteously at some poor sucker left standing and say, he did it, it's not our fault. Remind you of something?

Now, ask yourself, what kind of people will want to get into this business in the "private" sector? What incentive will they have? What time-scale will they have? I see MBAs, lawyers, former saving-and-loan managers, real-estate tycoons, and former politicians getting into it for the guaranteed tax revenue and for the opportunity to pick many pockets and you can bet they are planning to get out in five or six years, so they aren't left holding the bag.

Who benefits? Anybody between 70 and 100+ who is smart enough to play the game over the next decade. After that, nobody.

Who loses? Anybody who is not sick paying FICA and Medicare taxes plus premiums to some Don't-Care HMO over the next decade. After that, everybody. The hidden loss, of course, is the American health-care system itself, which is already and will continue quietly vanishing.

What can we do about it? Not a damned thing that I can see from here. Government controls the insurance industry and government controls the health-care industry. Exit government controls and maybe we can create an honest, durable, system. Go figure.

Update 1998.1: Some of the figures are in. Real gross domestic product (GDP) rose 4% in 1997. 37.7% of that growth went to taxes, never mind the total taxation, which is around 60%. At what point do we admit that we are slaves to the state? When 80% of your life is devoted to somebody else? 90%? Turn up the television, Martha, so I can't think.

Well, the Health Care Financing people who run Medicare and Medicaid are making louder and louder threats already this year and more and more professionals are bailing out. The Joint Commission on Accreditation of Hospitals, without whose seal of approval you cannot get paid at all, has noticed the alarming decline in services, the direct result of downsizing hospital staffs, and has changed tactics for accrediting hospitals. Heretofore, they have confined their Gestapo interrogations to department managers and medical records personnel. This year they are expanding their net to include actual patient-caregivers. This is a stop-you-in-the-hall-and-question-you procedure and you damned well better have the right answer or your hospital could be shut down, putting you out of work.

Thus we are required to memorize our "Mission Statement". Here is part of it:

"To be committed to serving the needs of our community by providing high quality health care with compassion and respect for the individual.

"To provide coordinated, seamless integration of holistic services and maintain a professional, state-of-the-art facility, while remaining ethically sensitive to each individual.

"To be dedicated to enhancing professional and spiritual growth while focusing on positive, customer driven outcomes."

If that makes any sense to you, you should not be reading this. This goes on for another three pages, in sixteen-point type so that some of the folks who can't read so well can mouth it into their brains, and I won't burden you with the rest.

The fact is, this is a very, very bad new year in hospitals; the flu virus that the National Institute of Health overlooked is killing people and those people are dying in woefully understaffed hospitals. Oh, we have plenty of managers, don't worry, it's the patient-caregivers who are missing. And these are the people who get stopped in mid-stride on some urgent errand to help somebody to recite this childish drivel.

Well, the bureaucrats are running scared, that much is plain, and they want the troops to promise to say that everything is okay. Say you have time to care, say it's high quality, say anything except the truth. The truth is, we are too overworked to care, we are too exhausted to care, there are too many really sick people and too few hands to help, because THEY destroyed the system.

My advice to you, gentle reader, is, don't get sick.

Update 1998.2: Lawyers practicing medicine for power and profit: While the Washington politicians and the AARP join hands to circumvent real Medicare reform and to yap endlessly about fraud, there are some real rats in the woodpile who are ripping off this system from the inside out.

Take the doctor whose peculiar specialty takes him to a multitude of nursing homes. First he locates a diabetic eighty-something patient who has lost a foot or two to the disease, then he calls his college buddy, the lawyer, and they go to work. The lawyer subpoenas the medical records and together they comb through them looking for a mistake. Believe me, we work very hard to keep mistakes out of medical records; in fact, as much attention is paid to medical records as to medical results. Still, there's always something. The lawyer then files a malpractice suit, usually against the primary family-practice physician in overall charge of the patient's care. The physician's malpractice insurance contacts the patient's lawyer to find out if the patient will settle out of court. Sure. Fifty-thousand. Fine. The patient gets thirty, the doctor and the lawyer get ten each. And everybody is happy: the patient gets some money, the doctor gets some money, the lawyer gets some money, and the family practice physician gets to go home without paying higher premiums—they never demand more than the magic limit set by liability insurance companies.

Why are the insurance companies willing to pay? Because a trial in court costs more than the payoff. Nobody got hurt and, besides, it's perfectly legal. So what's the problem? If you asked that question, I refer you to Henry Hazlitt's book, ***Economics in One Lesson.***

The second case I'd like to discuss involves a physician with whom I have worked for several years and for whom I have nothing but respect, Wolfgang Schug. You may have seen Dr. Schug on television, for this case attracted national attention. In a nutshell, Dr. Schug treated a child in the emergency room and the child subsequently died. With lawyers in cases like this, it's don't call us, we'll call you first. So a malpractice suit was filed. ***Eighteen months after*** the event, the lawyer representing the family took the case before the county grand jury and asked for a murder indictment. The grand jury complied. Suddenly the state attorney general's office appeared and took over the case. They arrested the doctor at work in the emergency room. Six months later the judge threw the case out of court for lack of evidence, the state had no case. His defense cost Dr. Schug $220,000.00—he sold everything except his home and he remains heavily in debt.

The malpractice suit was inevitable and would most likely have settled out of court for around $90,000. Then, last summer, something new entered the legal arena. Three nurses in Denver were indicted for murder by a grand jury; one nurse had accidentally overdosed an infant with an antibiotic solution prepared by a pharmacist (the pharmacist was not charged). This indictment stunned the world of nursing. I asked myself, what are the lawyers up to here? What is a grand jury indictment?

One of Dr. Schug's defense lawyers explained it to me like this: "The grand jury is the Star Chamber of the American legal system." Ah. The prosecution holds a trial, a one-sided trial, where the accused is not invited. Witnesses are grilled, evidence is presented, and the grand jury arrives at a verdict. The lawyer further told me that he could get a grand jury indictment against Mother Theresa for a murder committed two months after she died, no problem.

Okay, so the lawyers used a grand jury of ignorant laymen to indict the nurses in Denver and Dr. Schug here in California. Why? Because out of court settlements in malpractice cases are peanuts compared with a potential jury settlement in a malpractice case against a murderer. It's brilliant! Convict them of murder first, then sue them for malpractice. (Actually, you do it in the reverse order, but murder takes precedence.)

Why did the state attorney general's office jump into this case? Do you suppose it had anything to do with the election year? The governor's office? We had some mighty highly (tax) paid lawyers in our little rural courthouse. They tried to raise the bail—the judge lowered it. They tried to take the doctor's license—the judge denied it. Well, the judge didn't do this on his own. Dr. Schug had two, then three, highly (privately) paid, experienced, big-city lawyers of his own.

Meanwhile, the state attorney general's office had another issue on its agenda. They went after the "privileged" secrecy of the peer review process. Spawned by the legal profession's penetration of medical practice, peer review is a committee of doctors who review and judge the practice of their fellow doctors outside of any legal snooping. This, of course, deprives the vulture of his dead meat. This battle was fought in a higher court and, unfortunately, or inevitably, the battle was lost. Lawyers can now introduce peer review records as evidence in court, thus destroying any value of peer review and saddling all doctors with higher risk.

So what does this case prove? It proves that ALL of us who work in health-care professions can be indicted for murder. It proves that the state can and will crush and impoverish a private citizen in its quest for power.

I am proud of my work in health-care, but I am no longer proud to be working in health-care, I'm afraid of the job. I am afraid of these people. I am afraid of the cops, I am afraid of the lawyers, I am afraid of the courts, I am afraid of this government. I will retire soon, please hasten the day, and I wonder who will replace me? Who is blind enough to go into this risky health-care business?

"It's not justice, it's just court." (Bumper sticker)

Update 2000: I did not update this commentary in 1999 because the issues I had been highlighting for several years made front-page news all by themselves. The HMO fraud has proceeded as I predicted it would, although much more quickly than I had guessed. The easy money was ripped off and private enterprise was blamed for it. As a congressional patsy, it worked just dandy. There is an interesting analogy here with the fall-guys who took the hits for their beloved psychopath in the Oval Office, but I will restrain myself, that is not my subject here.

My personal venue changed last year from rural Northern California to urban Central Florida and with that change have come some new observations. Public perception of the dilemma posed by socialized medicine in Florida are roughly a decade behind California, that is, people in Florida still believe in the system. One reason for this is the substantial difference in the cost of operation; wages, for example, are twenty-five percent less in Florida. This difference is demonstrated by continuing capital improvements in physical facilities and by higher levels of staffing inside the facilities, both a mark of unjustified optimism which disappeared in California long ago. The difficult process of actually getting paid for work already done, reimbursement from Medicare and Medicaid, is still spoken about in whispers, like an embarrassing secret. The secret, however, is getting out.

**Here is an email that was forwarded to me by a friend:**

*From: Jean Elliott Brown on Sep 26, 2000 12:44 PM*
*Subject: Please Help Save $6.6 million for our Hospitals*
*To: info@jeanelliottbrown.com*

*Dear Friends and Supporters:*

*Will you lend a hand and help send a fax to Congressman Bill Archer so we can save $6.6 million in funding for our Treasure Coast hospitals? http://jeanelliottbrown.com/issues/medicare.php3*

*In the closing days of Congress, we have a problem with the Medicare reimbursement rates at the hospitals in Indian River, St. Lucie, and Martin Counties, Florida. One hospital missed the deadline to submit its wage data, which is required for the calculation of the 2001 Medicare reimbursement schedule. This error impacts the hospitals starting October 1 (next week). It hasn't been fixed yet and some of the hospitals have already started to announce cutbacks and one is closing its facility for a 17-year-old midwifery program for poor mothers. All this because of a reporting problem in one of the hospitals.*
*The hospitals are:*
*Lawnwood Regional Medical Center in Ft. Pierce, FL*
*Indian River Memorial Hospital in Vero Beach*
*St. Lucie Medical Center in Port St. Lucie*
*Martin Memorial Medical Center in Stuart*

*Newspaper reports indicate they will collectively receive $6.6 million less in reimbursement over the next year because of this error.*

*The error cannot be corrected administratively...it requires an act of Congress...a one-sentence amendment to an appropriations bill. The incumbent Representatives have not fixed this problem to date, so I have suggested legislation for inclusion in an appropriate bill and have contacted Senator Bob Graham's office. Senator Graham's office is working on the issue from their side of Congress. We need help in the House. Now, at this late date, there are only seven days left in this session of Congress and there is some (ok, a lot of) resistance to last minute amendments such as this. But these are real and immediate cutbacks due solely to an administrative problem at one hospital, yet all will be forced to cut back. Would you please send a fax Chairman Bill Archer of the House Ways & Means Committee now and ask him to include this amendment? He is the man with the power to make it happen.*

*This will take you right to the link, just type in your name and we will send the fax off right away.*
*http://jeanelliottbrown.com/issues/medicare.php3*

*Please e-mail this to any of your friends in the area, it doesn't matter what party they are, this should be a non-partisan issue. Lets get the word out and show Chairman Archer just how many people will appreciate his efforts on this issue. Remember, we only have a week, after that, we all lose if the hospitals have to cut back almost $7 million in services now offered.*

*Thank you again for all of your support. Now lets see how fast we can spread the word.*

*Jean Elliott Brown*

*Democratic Nominee for US Congress*
*Florida District 16*
*http://jeanelliottbrown.com*
*jean@jeanelliottbrown.com*

In Florida, apparently, an aspirant to political power does not question the central government's power to authorize the collection of "wage data" from an institution in a vassal state. On another level, however, this appeal to the public reveals the kind of fine-tuning of reimbursement policy that's going on in Washington, fine-tuning intended to stop spending tax-money on health-care in ways that continue to lay the blame for failure on local care-providers and not on the central government, where the total blame belongs. Politicians are very, very good at this shell-game and people simply don't have time to watch every move they make.

Admitted or not, talked about or not, socialized health-care in Southeastern America is in the same precarious jeopardy as it is in Western America. Here in Florida, good people proceeding in good faith from day to day have not yet had their faces rubbed in the harsh reality of the financial failure of local health-care facilities, but they will, Washington is working on it. I wonder who they will blame when it happens?

# Cash Only

## A Story

## 1997

### Dedicated to Wolgang Schug, M.D.

College degrees, certificates, licenses, and endorsements lined the east wall of the office. Her eyes flicked from one walnut frame to the other, counting. Bachelors from Indiana, four years, $40,000.00. Masters from Ohio, two years $20,000.00. M.D., New York, three years, $45,000.00. Residency, New York, two years, $25,000.00. Add it up. Eleven years, $130,000, and don't count the crummy apartments, the junk cars, the raggedy clothes, the cheap food, the ruined friendships, and all the fun. What the hell is fun? She had sacrificed the decade of her twenties in one relentless drive to become a Family Practitioner. And it was not fun.

She looked down at the piece of paper. It wasn't even addressed to her personally. It just said, Dear Doctor. Medicare was cutting back her reimbursement by another ten percent. She thought about the hundred-grand in student loans left to pay off, about her apartment rent, car payment, office rent, office supplies, insurance, wages and benefits to her front office girl and to her back office girl, to her office manager and her billing clerk, these girls who could afford to buy better clothes than she could, and her gross income. Maybe one-twenty this year. Were the hundred-hour weeks really worth it?

She sighed, pushed away from the desk, and looked up at the wall once more. Medical Doctor. Doctor Christopher. Doctor Leah Christopher. Yes! It was worth it.

She arrived at the Medical Staff Meeting as the steam tables rolled into the room. Dinner time.

"How's it going, Leah?"

"Pretty good, Stan," she replied to the lanky Chief of Staff, Stanley Goldberg. Stan was an internist, an easy going, friendly guy who had been in practice for twenty years.

"Think I have time to see patients?" she asked.

"Sure," Stan smiled, "we're pretty easy here."

She had counted on a fifty-percent reduction in her student loans by locating her practice in a rural community, but there was some hang-up in Washington and she was still making payments on the full amount. Still, she liked the countryside and she liked the little hospital and its staff. In a way, beginning her practice in a small town was a dream come true.

"...and I don't think it's our problem, Stan."

They were conducting business over spaghetti and garlic buns when she returned. Morris St. James, the urologist, held up a fork and whined in his high-pitched voice, "None of us had anything to do with this case and besides, he's a contractor."

"Which is beside the point," Rhudy Anderson countered, "he's a doctor and he has been wrongly accused. We need to stand behind him."

"He made a bad mistake."

"How do you know? Have you read the chart?"

"It's been subpoenaed, nobody can read it."

"Well, he must have made a bad mistake or they wouldn't have arrested him."

"You've got a lot of faith in the courts, Bud."

Anna Martinez stood up. Even in heels she only stood five feet, but she had presence. Silence fell on the group.

"You are missing the point here, gentlemen, and Doctor Christopher," she nodded toward Leah, the only other woman in the room, "they have taken a routine malpractice suit before a Grand Jury, tried Doctor Mann in secret and without his knowledge or defense, found him guilty of second-degree murder, and handed down a formal indictment. This procedure, and I emphasize the word procedure, has never been followed before in a case like this. If this procedure is allowed to stand uncontested, then we are all of us, every single person working in health-care professions, in extreme jeopardy. That is why we must support his legal defense."

After a moment of silence, Doctor Goldberg said, "Thank you, Doctor Martinez. Now I will take a motion."

As the Medical Staff voted to contribute to the legal defense fund, Doctor Leah Christopher munched on her green beans and tried to remember what she had heard. They had had a very sick child in the emergency room who needed a pediatric intensivist. Air transport could not fly and ground transport was already out of county. The parents had insisted they could drive to the Medical Center themselves. They did, but when they arrived, the child was comatose and soon died. Now they were suing the doctor for malpractice and for murder. That's all she knew. As for Anna's statement, she didn't know what to think. She didn't know anything about law or about legal procedures. Yet it made sense. If they could accuse Doctor Mann of murder, they could accuse any of them of murder.

She caught up with Anna on the front steps after the meeting. "So this thing with Sebastian is really bad," she said.

Anna looked up at her. "Yes, it is. The State Attorney General would like to get a ride to the Governor's Mansion on this case. The feds got involved thanks to the anti-dumping statutes that regulate transport. So we've got a lot of tax-paid professionals going after him."

"Can't we do something more for him?"

Doctor Martinez glanced into her eyes, then looked away. "Leah, I don't know what more we can do for Sebastian, but I do know I have some advice for you."

"For me?" Leah was surprised.

"We all admire you for coming here, Leah, this isn't exactly an exciting place for a young doctor. But I think you're making a mistake by opening a solo practice. You'd be a lot safer in a group."

Leah felt the anger flash, but she contained it. Martinez was old enough to be her grandmother, almost, and she meant well. "Anna, I don't know how to say this," she began, "but when I was growing up, I decided to become a doctor with my own private practice in a small town like this. That's what I am and that's what I'm going to be."

The older woman smiled faintly. "And you're going to do well, Leah." She patted the young woman's arm and wished her goodnight.

Newspaper headlines announced that the Community Hospital was being investigated for Medicare fraud, that Medicare was taking back two-million dollars in overpayments, and that the hospital faced bankruptcy. The CFO explained to the Board of Directors that Medicare had changed several hundred code numbers five years ago and that many of the new ones had not been entered into their computer correctly, which meant that they wound up billing for the wrong things. The Board took that into consideration and fired the CFO. The real problem that they faced was an aging population which required more and more care at the same time that reimbursement for that care was steadily declining. Costs up, income down. To significantly reduce costs they would necessarily have to break dozens of state and federal laws regulating hospitals. As one of the Board members said, "We might just as well close the joint and be done with it."

Early Intervention International, Inc., a conglomerate listed on the New York Stock Exchange which bought, sold, traded, and closed hospitals, home-health agencies, durable medical equipment companies, and medical supply manufacturers, came to town and negotiated with the Board to buy the Community Hospital.

The idea that they might be ruled from a boardroom in New York panicked the Medical Staff. They convened an emergency executive committee meeting at one member's home, then called some friends in the state capitol and some more friends at the Medical Center. The Medical Center agreed in principle that they might be interested in buying the Community Hospital if the physicians would, in turn, sell their single and group practices to the Medical Center, thus ensuring that patients who needed specialized care would not be sent elsewhere.

Leah arrived home exhausted. She went to the refrigerator and poured a glass of milk, then slumped on the couch facing a blank television screen. She had worked half the night before with an elderly lady hospitalized with congestive heart failure, then all day at the office seeing four or five patients an hour, then back to the hospital and, finally, she had spent two grueling hours with her accountant. The bottom line was, she couldn't make it. Her overhead was too high, her income was too low. Charging her patients fifty-five dollars per visit wasn't enough and she couldn't charge more. Her accountant said, sell out, buy yourself a nice house and a new car, pay off your debts, take the time to meet somebody, get married, raise a family. You don't have to work like this for nothing.

She roused herself and spread the papers out on the coffee table. She hunched over them, searching for an answer. All of her life people had been telling her what she couldn't do. She couldn't go to college, then she did. She couldn't go to graduate school, then she did. She'd never make it through medical school, then she did. She wouldn't survive residency and she did. Now they were telling her that she couldn't practice medicine as an independent entity. There had to be a way.

She awoke in the early morning with a bad taste in her mouth. While she was brushing her teeth, it came to her. She rushed into the living room, picked up pencil and paper and started figuring.

She could move out of this expensive apartment and rent one of the tumble-down houses on the east side. She could get rid of her fairly-new, used car and buy a clunker. She could say goodbye to her staff and move out of her expensive office. She could resign from the hospital staff and throw away her Medicare provider number. Yes! She could do it!

Dr. Martinez felt so sorry for the young woman, but she had warned her, after all. Still, it was one thing to be shunned by your peers, and quite another to be rejected by your mentor. So she drove along the dusty street looking for the address. There, a little white cottage with red shutters, a picket fence, and a small garden. An ancient sedan stood in the drive. She parked her Lexus and walked to the door. She read the sign:

Leah Christopher, M.D.
Family Practice

No Medicare
No Medicaid
No Insurance
No HMOs
Accepted

$20.00

**CASH ONLY**

# Don't Vote!

## 1998

Voting in political government is akin to driving the getaway car in a robbery, the voter is an accessory to a crime. In the case of political government, the crime is coercion against individuals carried out by the armed force which stands behind every political law, every political lawmaker, and every political institution. Unlike the world of free-markets, in political government when some individuals win, other individuals lose.

We allow the state to teach our children that majority rule in political government is good, proper, and fair. The state does not teach our children that the authors of the Constitution were mortally afraid of majority rule and that they expended every effort to prevent it, an effort which was subsequently subverted. The state does not teach our children that when a majority rules, a minority is ruled. The concept of political democracy was flawed at its birth in ancient Greece and has remained flawed ever since precisely because a majority of people elect which self-interest will be enforced by arms, which ultimately and inevitably leads to the use of those self-same arms against the majority, the minority, and every living thing in sight. It is no accident that the fantasies which we have been taught by the state are now enabling a domestic army to be used against us; history teaches us that this is inevitable.

For thirty years I have wondered which President of the United States will be our last one, for history also teaches us that a majority in political democracy will elect a tyrant to rule, to solve the millions of problems which political government created and democracy cannot solve. Every President recognizes this and watches for the opportunity, our idols of Lincoln, FDR, and Kennedy being no exception whatsoever. The state would like us to forget that the Germans elected Hitler. Each President has gathered power to the office for two centuries, slowly at first, quickly these days, so that the office may create its own disaster, dissolve congress, and come to our rescue exactly as Hitler did, then give us the option of electing him as tyrant, which will be no option at all.

Americans have always been busy people preoccupied with their own lives and they pay remarkably little attention to what our full-time political government is really doing, which is creating and passing more and more laws which restrict our personal liberty and curtail our commerce. It has been our singular ability to create wealth faster than our political government can destroy it which has kept the predatory state at bay and allowed us to live with our illusions of freedom, liberty, and justice. The facts do not support this happy condition, however. Who is going to pay for entitlements in thirty years? Who is going to pay off government bonds in thirty years? With a total taxation rate of sixty-percent of wealth produced annually TODAY, what will it be in thirty years? The question is not, what is going to happen, the question is, when?

We are simply repeating the history of mankind, the true history, not the wishful ignorance of state schoolteachers. We have been conned into standing on the scaffold with the noose around our necks, the rope looped over political government, with the bitter end in our own hands, waiting to be told to hang on tight and jump. This is voting in political government; this voluntary suicide is the crime, a crime against life, a crime against nature. Don't do it. Don't vote!

# Your Vote Counts!

## 2000

Your vote counts in the marketplace, where your dollar elects goods and services. Your vote also counts in political government, where your ballot elects force and fraud.

The United States of America was founded on the rule of law, not of men. Factions and special interests were supposed to give way to justice before the law. But men make political law and special interests broke the rules before the ink was dry on the Constitution, commercial tariffs and the theft of Indian land being first on the agenda.

The rule of law is dead. Jefferson warned of this outcome in a democracy—the history of mankind was not an unrevealed mystery to men like him. Throughout the Nineteenth and the Twentieth Centuries other men warned and then lamented the passing of a noble ideal. The men in power lie, cheat, murder, and steal at will, in the name of democracy, unrestrained by law. We all know that. We also know that there is nothing we can do about it, except vote, of course. Your vote assures them of their power, your vote sanctions their crimes.

Still, I wonder, is this social system of political government really a democracy, as the politicians and the media constantly insist? In the year 2000, only one-third of the United States population voted at all.

What does this mean? Does it mean that two-thirds of the population don't care? I don't think so.

Some folks talk about secession again, apparently meaning that some states or regions could drop out of the consolidated union as a political protest against the central power. Under the circumstances, I view this proposal as an invitation to another Civil War. Maybe that's what they want. I don't see the choice between one political government over another political government to be any choice at all, we'd still end up with political government—a social system with a hundred-percent perfect rate of failure. Yet the idea of secession might explain what happened to the silent two-thirds of our population who did not vote in this loudly proclaimed political democracy.

I doubt if there is a significant number of Americans who flat refuse to vote, not yet anyway, and I imagine that most Americans who do not vote shrug it off as irrelevant to their lives. The media calls it apathy. What is apathy? The dictionary says it's "lack of interest or concern." What would cause a lack of interest or concern in two-thirds of the American population? Something about government? What would it be reasonable to suppose that Americans know for sure about their political government?

Taxes. Income taxes, property taxes, sales taxes, excise taxes, money taken from people against their will under the threat of force. Foreign wars, inexplicable and inexcusable use of force abroad, with the threat of the military draft not forgotten. Domestic wars, inexplicable and inexcusable use of force against our fellow citizens; Wounded Knee, Kent State, Ruby Ridge, and Waco come to mind as well as guns, tobacco, marijuana, and alcohol. Despicable politicians, with the exposed public lies of Nixon, Reagan, and Clinton most conspicuous, but with a legion of others merely forgotten under the sheer volume of them. Isn't that enough? But let's not forget the deep and widespread certainty that the big-ticket political promises, Social Security and Medicare, will fail in our lifetime.

Political government consists of force and fraud, it doesn't take a rocket scientist to figure that out. Two-thirds of our population do not approve and do not vote. That's secession. When the same two-thirds discover a way to hide their money from political government, we may learn just how much our vote—in the marketplace—really does count.

# ELECTION 2000

## 2000

I oppose voting in political elections, where any vote is always cast for coercion—which I don't want; I support voting in the marketplace, where any vote is always cast for goods and services—which I do want. Normally I ignore political elections, but Election 2000 has been too interesting to ignore, interesting because the post-election process has exposed every false premise underlying political government, beginning with the propaganda lie, it's your government. Sorry folks, it isn't yours, it's theirs, you just pay for it.

I have no interest in the outcome of this or of any political election, but I am keenly interested in the processes of force and fraud that keep nearly every one of us under surveillance and obedient to the rules of the state, the primary purpose of which is to collect taxes to pay for the power to enforce the processes of force and fraud. Social welfare schemes are all a variation of any pyramid racket, while the justice system is a variation of any protection racket. The crooks at the top skim off as much as they can, while the crooks at the bottom try to get to the top. Nothing new there, that's political government.

What's new in the wake of this election is the apparent confusion amongst the certified or self-appointed intellectuals to explain what it means and what it portends. In rough figures, one-third of the American population voted and two-thirds of the American population did not vote. Of the one-third who did vote, half went one way and half went the other way and that is ALL that the intellectuals will talk about or write about. What about the two-thirds who did not vote? Does the majority of the American population have no intellectual voice to speak for it? Here is something new.

Some few intellectuals are beginning to whisper that the American people seem to be fed up with big government, like they're guessing the sun might rise tomorrow. Yes, I'd say that's a fact we can safely rely upon. We are fed up with government, big and little, with its guns and intrusions and endless taxation.

Some few intellectuals are beginning to whisper that the American people might be happier if we rolled back the government clock to, say, 1800, when it only murdered a few people for refusing to pay taxes. Okay, like how? How do you convince the crook he would be better off with less ransom? How do you keep me from thinking, why should I pay the ransom? Do I really need the crook?

I'm nobody's intellectual, but I'll venture my own guess that two-thirds of the American population are watching this charade, like me, and laughing at it, like me, convinced that we don't need political government at all. I think we'll get what we want. I think we'll end up with free-market elections for security, justice, and individual liberty just as soon as we laugh these crooks out of business.

# Imperialism:
# Decline and Fall of the USA

## 1999

*Imperialism* is defined in Webster's Ninth New Collegiate Dictionary as: 1: imperial government, authority, or system; 2: the policy, practice, or advocacy of extending the power and dominion of a nation esp. [sic] by direct territorial acquisitions or by gaining indirect control over the political or economic life of other areas.

When I was young and twenty, some forty-years ago, I scoffed at the Communist accusation that the USA had imperialist ambitions. I truly believed, as I was taught to believe, that the intentions of the USA were righteous and honorable, that we were, somehow, the Lone Ranger defending the weak and liberating the enslaved.

Ah, but time passes and I watched our wars in Korea (unresolved), Viet Nam (lost), Grenada (war?), Iraq (unresolved), Bosnia (unresolved), and now in Yugoslavia (unresolved), not to mention the innumerable interjections of USA military forces in South America and Africa, and I wonder what those who exercise this kind of power have in mind? Is the exercise of power an exercise unto itself? Or are we watching the transformation of political democracy into an imperial state?

Americans have a history of disagreeing with their political government, our founding fathers rebelled against their own government, after all. In modern times our government has responded to our disagreement in disagreeable ways: Kent State, Wounded Knee, Ruby Ridge, Waco, and the endless persecution of potential troublemakers for smoking marijuana and the equally endless persecution of ordinary citizens by the IRS.

I will not mince words, every USA President since Lincoln has searched for a way to become emperor and none has succeeded. Yet. Today we happen to have in that office the consummate and defining psychopath who challenges the historical model of tyrants throughout history; here is a man who would be emperor. He has the power.

This is an historic time. Political government has always failed, political government has failed 100% of the time, political government is failing again. Political democracy has always devolved into tyranny and it is doing so again, under our noses and with our money. What can we do?

Armed rebellion is out of the question this time, nobody can stand up to the USA military. Political protest may succeed in a temporary delay of the inevitable simply because "they" can't kill everybody and still expect to eat (they know that). Still, this system will fail. So what can we do?

First, seek knowledge, knowledge of the past, knowledge of the present. Second, consider, in the light of knowledge, an alternative paradigm, or model, for government. There is an alternative. Whether we have the time to initiate a new paradigm for government or whether we may survive in the attempt is irrelevant, to quit trying is unthinkable.

If we take our lives seriously, if we care about the future of mankind, we owe it to ourselves to think and to search for the truth. Why should we cling to a system which has never worked? Why can't we create something better? We can.

# Where Have All The Boomers Gone?

## 1999

### Written during the bombing of Belgrade

I am speaking about that generation of Americans who were born of WWII, who grew up during the Cold War and the constant threat of nuclear annihilation, who fought and died in Vietnam and at Kent State. Where have they gone?

This I am wondering as we approach our first National Fishing Holiday of the summer, officially called Memorial Day: Memorial to the thousands upon thousands of American lives sacrificed in this Twentieth Century of our reckoning to political war. Didn't the BOOMERS decide that they had had enough of this barbaric method of doing things? Didn't the BOOMERS decide to erect a Memorial to their sacrificed peers? Have the BOOMERS cried their hearts out for that particular waste of time, energy, money, and lives in our political history?

So many tears have they cried that they have none left to cry for their own children who are about to be sacrificed in yet another waste of time, energy, money, and lives. Their Memorial is a sham, their generation is a fraud, their silence is shameful, where have they gone?

# Wising Up

## 1999

As cynical and pessimistic about political government as I am, I see that I am learning something worse about it than I would have guessed not long ago.

I never paid much attention to Vietnam, I was too busy working and raising a family, but during the bombing of Iraq I got to thinking about what we did to that region and the legacy we left there in the form of unexploded bombs, like the things that continue to kill and maim children in Vietnam, Cambodia, and Laos thirty years later. In retrospect, I see we were then and still are intent on utterly destroying a population.

I have no idea how much central planning went into tricking Saddam into invading Kuwait and then turning it into a fine little war, again waged against the population. I didn't think about what the people might be doing for essentials like shelter, food, and water while we steadily destroyed their Twentieth Century infrastructure and sent them back to the Thirteenth Century where starvation and pestilence and disease kept people in line.

Now I believe this manufactured war in Yugoslavia is finally wising me up. First all the hype about the BAD GUY, the same old copy of Ho and Saddam with a startling new name. Suddenly we can forget about the man who lies under oath, the man who sells state secrets to the enemy, the man who rapes, pillages, and murders in his own playing fields, the man who conquers the US Senate, and we can watch his fine little war.

Only this one isn't so fine. So-called military objectives were never announced and the bombing of the civilian infrastructure began immediately. Maybe the Germans still hold a grudge against these people for pinning down twenty-two German divisions for the duration of WWII. Maybe the English still lust for days of turning a country into a used-brick market. Maybe Europe is tired of this region's ages old ethnic conflict and just wants to shut them up for good.

Consider what destroying the water supply to Belgrade means. It means they can't drink water, it means they can't wash themselves or their clothes, and it means they can't flush their toilets. It is the last consequence that bothers me the most. They can probably find something else to drink for a while and they can live in dirty clothes, but their sewage will kill them.

We have littered the cities and the countryside with explosive devices which maim and kill animals and children. As in Iraq, we are using spent uranium shells which poison the soil and the air, so those who survive the bombs are looking at death from cancer.

The US President has exceeded the authority of the War Powers Act and the Congress bows to whatever threats they bowed to not long ago. The press is silent, this is their President, after all. What is this country doing?

It finally came to me this afternoon. Vietnam taught our political state a lesson. Don't screw around with these people, get in there and kill them all. Hark, the herald sings, don't waste time with a Wounded Knee, wipe them out with a Waco. Don't fiddle around with a Vietnam, destroy the whole population. And that is what we are doing.

Dear God, what next? Miami?

# Who Won What War?

## 1999

Katarina reports from Belgrade <http://www.wardiary.org> that the bombing of the civilian population in that city has stopped. WorldNetDaily.com reports that the Serbian army is withdrawing from Kosovo while NATO forces are preparing to move in. Is the war over? If so, who won?

The President of Yugoslavia is claiming victory. The British Prime Minister is claiming victory. The NATO generals are claiming victory. The US President is claiming victory. Looks like a win-win situation all around. Are we now to get that fuzzy feel-good feeling that the old Victory At Sea movies were supposed to promote? Desert Storm Heros Win Again?

I don't think so. I don't think we have anything to be proud about or happy about. I do think we have a gargantuan problem facing us. Political government won this war, his political government, their political government, our political government, and the people lost it—bought it, paid for it, and lost it.

Murdering civilians in the interest of political power is nothing new, as the Christian Old Testament makes abundantly clear. Later, Attila the Hun and his descendants notified folks who was boss with pyramids of human skulls, a message any illiterate could read. Today we use smart bombs and pilots stupid enough to deliver them, cluster bombs to kill the children, cows, and goats, shell casings made of "spent uranium" to poison the soil and to continue killing with cancer. The message here is, murder the civilian population and political government wins.

This war was said to be about a nasty military aggression in a small rural territory called Kosovo. Belgrade is not in Kosovo. NATO bombed Belgrade. NATO destroyed the water supply, food supply, electrical supply, communications and transportation facilities of a civilian city to achieve...what? Political dominance? Well, that they did. Only the people died for it and, as NATO says, they don't count.

What does count? If the people living their everyday lives in a given region don't count, what does count? If the people of Baghdad and the people of Belgrade don't count, then the people of London and the people of San Francisco don't count either. What does count?

To quote Steve Foerster, "Who needs political government?" We don't need them, they need us, the people who don't count. We, the people, lost another war.

# In the Name of Law and Order

## 1999

What is a militia? Webster's Ninth New Collegiate Dictionary defines militia: *1: A part of the organized armed forces of a country liable to call only in emergency; 2: The whole body of able-bodied male citizens declared by law as being subject to call to military service.*

In this era of political-speak and double-talk, where common words take on new—or no—meaning, it's hard to know what our government means by militia. By definition, the National Guard is a militia. By definition, a wartime male population subject to military draft "by law" is a militia. But when our government declares it will take preemptive measures against American militia in preparation for the Y2K social disruption for which they pray, I believe they do not mean to paralyze themselves, which would be a blessing for all of us, but to paralyze private citizens with imprisonment without accusation or trial and to murder select citizens who oppose their tyranny with a loud voice.

The tepid excuse for mobilizing troops within American civil jurisdictions for "maneuvers" this past year has routinely been terrorism. Whose terrorism? Up until now, it's been "theirs" whoever "they" are. Arabs? Albanians? Serbs? Chinese? North Korean? Are the Chinese going to blow up a shopping center in Durham, North Carolina? What kind of fools do they take us for?

If the entire technological world is brought to a halt at midnight, January 1, 2000, how are these dreadful terrorists going to get around any better than the rest of us? Do they have some secret magic that we don't have? Flying camels? Maybe?

Now the latest excuse to terrorize OUR OWN civilian population is the threat of American militia. Evidently they mean armed Americans who are not wearing a uniform or subject to a draft, i.e., exactly the opposite of the definition; plus, they also mean conspiracies, like five guys complaining about taxes over a poker game. Or how about five-million people complaining about our government's policies, lies, and extortions over the Internet? Five million people can be silenced. Easy. The Germans did it over fifty years ago and they didn't even have access to everybody's email (for you youngsters, there wasn't any email back then).

If there are conspiracies, they are few and ineffectual, like the petty crooks in Montana a few years ago who were called a militia. But terrorist and militia are hot-button, big time words these days with the media; I wonder if they are writing the script on the Y2K hysteria? If the government can depend on its media to justify its murders abroad, can it also depend on its media to justify its murders at home? Apparently it can.

As the clock ticks into the computers' millennium, we may encounter a few disruptions, which is reasonable considering mankind's short-sighted nature, but the terrorists and the militia we have to fear the most belong to our own government.

# On Democracy

## 1998

The one simple and undeniable fact of history is: All civilizations have failed. Historians in all places and times have acknowledged this fact and some have painstakingly tried to explain it. Without fail, they ignore the use to which each and every political government put its monopoly on coercion. As my mentor, Andrew J. Galambos, said, "There are only two political parties at any given time, the INS and the OUTS. The OUTS want to get IN and the INS want to stay IN." Coercion becomes the arbiter, the people are enslaved to the purpose, the wars begin, and another Dark Age ensues. What is at fault, unrecognized, is the political paradigm of government itself, i.e., political government does not work.

The true foundations of any civilization are innovation and free-trade, which necessarily imply liberty, security, and justice amongst the people living at the time. Government is called upon to supply the demand for liberty, security, and justice so that innovation and free-trade may flourish. The question of government becomes: How can we supply that demand without coercive political government?

The answer lies in economic democracy. I vote with my dollar; I vote for a telephone company, I vote for a cable company, I vote for software companies, I vote for my Internet Service Provider. I would similarly vote for liberty, security, and justice companies—if they existed!

What I call Economic Government consists of three interlocking, private, profit-seeking institutions which are, simply, insurance, banking, and innovation clearinghouse. Properly structured, these institutions would be capable of selling absolute liberty, security, and justice without the need for coercion.

However, not only do these institutions not exist in the form that I envision, they would not be permitted to exist by political government, no more than King George could permit an assault on his authority. But we have the technology to circumvent our petty kings, the Internet.

The Internet represents existential democracy and intellectual liberty undreamed of in all of history. Even in its present chaotic condition it is a threat to all political governments on this planet. Our very first imperative must be to ensure that our American political government does not tax or restrain our use of the Internet in any way, shape, or form, including attacks on hardware and software innovation. If we lose this battle, we lose the war.

Assuming we win, the opportunity will exist to increasingly turn money into anonymous electronic digits and to carry on business on the Internet, encrypted, of course, and the opportunity will exist to establish the institutions of Economic Government. Then government will be truly vested in the supreme power of the people and only then will true democracy begin.

# Who Owns What?

## 1999

Andrew J. Galambos said that people could resolve most disputes by asking this simple question, who owns what? He liked to chuckle over the example of a child's toys littering the floor: When the parent tells the child to pick up the toys, the child says, "But they're my toys!" To which the parent responds, "Yes, but they're on my floor."

Answering this question outside of the privacy of one's home is not so simple, we have the "public" to deal with. Who is the public? You, me, everybody, and nobody. The public doesn't exist, only the concept of the public exists and it is represented by the individuals who constitute political government, i.e., the public is represented by the state. If you want to know what the public owns, you have to ask the state.

I would have to ask a scholar about the origin of this concept, because I don't know for sure. I suppose it derives from our gregarious nature as human beings and dates back to the earliest creation of tools and shelters and the use of fire. Whose fire is it? Later I suppose small groups of people enclosed their dwellings with some kind of fences or walls to keep some animals in and other animals out. Did anybody ask, whose fence is it? I suppose not, it was a public works project for the good of the public.

In the late Eighteenth Century our founding fathers codified the paternalistic concept of "general welfare" and handed the responsibility for it to their new political government, thus paving the way for the megalithic state which claims to own us all today.

I had a long-winded discussion of economic government with a professor of political science, excuse the oxymoron, wherein the professor objected to the absence of institutions designed to provide for the general welfare. I, in turn, asked for a definition of general welfare. General welfare can only be defined by the state, which represents the general public, and there is no definition for it in economic government where there is no public and there is no state, there are only individual people who relate to one another by contractual agreement based on the definition of property. The professor insisted that the individual was subordinate to the general welfare, no matter what, so I asked, who owns you?

The professor was claiming that the public existed and was claiming to be a member of the public and was claiming to be a representative of the public as an individual public servant, that is, as an individual employed by the state to teach political science. The professor represented the public as a representative of the state and the professor therefore defined the general public welfare in the professor's best self-interests. The circularity of the argument led me to the question, who owns what? Does the professor own the public? Does the public own the professor? Or is ownership itself not a real issue? Or shall we let the state decide?

Galambos defined property as an individual's life and all non-procreative derivatives of that life, including innovation and wealth. Regarding human life as property lost popularity after machines replaced human slave labor, yet it is instructive to do so. If I view my life as my property, then the question of who owns my life takes on new meaning; if I own my life as my property, then I control my life as my property. I can invest my life in activities of my choice and take the gains or losses as my own. This is the fundamental principle of economic government, I own my life.

Out in the world of political government and public welfare, I do not own my life, the state owns my life. There are political laws on the books (compulsory education, military draft, zoning, taxation, etc.), backed up with guns and the threat of death, that inform me of this, for the benefit of the public welfare, as defined by the state which holds the guns. Is there any man, woman, or child, is there one human being on this planet who is not similarly owned by the state? We are all slaves to the general public welfare.

The professor believes this is a desirable condition; the professor's income depends on it. I did suggest that the professor could charge a suitable fee and then offer a money-back-guarantee on political science lectures, thus eliminating the immediate need for the state, as Galambos did, and the professor declined. I wonder why?

With economic government we can accomplish two things: We can eliminate coercion as viable human behavior and we can clearly establish who owns what. In fact, the two go hand in hand; the state can only destroy the distinction of who owns what with its monopoly on coercion. Eliminate coercion and who owns what becomes obvious: I own myself, you own yourself; I own my innovations, you own your innovations; I own my wealth, you own your wealth. Only by knowing exactly who owns what can the general welfare of individual human beings in society be assured.

# Objectivism:
# A Syntactical Review

## 1995

Certain words in the English language are so charged with emotional connotation that a speaker or writer using them risks losing the meaning of his sentence in the turmoil created by his words. Thus morals, morality, passion, passionate, ethics, ethical, virtue, virtuous, and purity are words that carry a burden of many meanings in the Christian culture we live in. Altering the definition of such words does nothing to alter the impact of their use in the English speaking world. One wonders, then, why the sole proponents of rational, logical thinking deliberately choose the syntax of their bible pounding competitors for the mind of mankind. I intend to review herein the syntax of a brief essay within one chapter of one book—the selection represents a good example of my thesis—*Objectivism: The Philosophy of Ayn Rand* by Leonard Peikoff, New York, Dutton 1991: Chapter 8, "Virtue", "Productiveness as the Adjustment of Nature to Man," pp. 298—303.

"Life is a process of goal-directed action."

That is a truism, an axiom, by the law of identity. The author calls this "purpose" and then calls it a "moral" value and then calls it a "principle".

"The principle of purpose means conscious goal-directedness in every aspect of one's existence where choice applies."

By definition, he rules out unconscious goal-directedness, a reality he does not address, and goal-directedness imposed by circumstances where choices still apply, but are not reasonable, i.e., I chose to feed and clothe my children rather than write a novel; "one can choose among higher-level alternatives only by reference to some end one seeks to attain." "Higher-level" choices, in my case, were kids or career, a common choice in today's world.

"Whether in regard to work or friends, love or art, entertainment or vacations, he knows what he likes and why, then goes after it."

I can confirm the truth of this statement from experience except in regard to work. You can choose your friends, love, art, etc., but you can't always choose your work; sometimes one takes what one can find.

"He is the person with a passionate ambition for *values* who wants every moment and step of his life to count in their service. Such a person does not resent the effort which purpose imposes. He enjoys the fact that the objects he desires are not given to him, but must be achieved. In his eyes, purpose is not drudgery or duty, but something good. The process of pursuing values is itself a value."

Here the strident catechism begins. I totally agree with his statement and I can verify that it is true, but why does he use the word "passionate" when a word like "dedicated" would express the concept dispassionately? What's to get passionate about? A clean house enables a clean computer which enables uninterrupted work, but that doesn't mean that I clean the house passionately.

"The principle of purpose sanctions deliberate rest or relaxation, but condemns a course of drifting or of inaction."

This syntax is puzzling. Let's look at the word "sanction": sanc·tion *tr.v.* sanc·tioned, sanc·tion·ing, sanc·tions. 1. To give official authorization or approval to. 2. To encourage or tolerate by indicating approval.

In the sense of official authorization, the use of this verb is provocative. Does the principle of purpose authorize behavior? Is it official? The implication here is that there is an authority behind the principle who approves or disapproves of some action. He sounds like a new Moses writing a new commandment. He implies that rest and relaxation are not the same as drifting or inaction. Come now, when asleep the resting mind is both drifting and inactive.

But note the word "course." "It condemns any form of being moved through one's days by the power of accident, such as a man's falling into a job, an affair, a philosophy..." Now we have the principle and the authority behind the principle condemning behavior and, remember, condemnation implies punishment. Again, we have the inflammatory harangue of the born-again true believer. What for? It's like a physics professor exhorting his students not to fall up. The drugged and dazed welfare recipients who the government is using to destroy the Bill of Rights and to bankrupt the middle-class will never read this, will never hear this, will shortly die from well-deserved starvation anyway, so why does he use this biblical syntax on people like me? And again, falling into an affair and falling into a philosophy are not the same as falling into a job; after the government destroys my profession, I will earnestly fall into any job I can find.

"A man with a hodgepodge of goals cannot achieve or even rationally pursue them." This is not true. A man can hold any number of dissimilar goals and achieve each one by rational pursuit.

"There is no way (besides caprice) for him to decide how to apportion his time and other assets among his concerns, or to decide how to resolve the conflicting demands in these regards." This is not true. Apportioning time to different goals is elementary; anybody can work for a living, study some unrelated subject, and civilize children if they want to spend the effort. Conflicting demands are common and are resolved as they arise. Either the author has had no experience of this kind or he has an ulterior motive for asserting "there is no way."

"A central purpose is the long-range goal that constitutes the primary claimant on a man's time, energy, and resources."

"A central purpose is the ruling standard of a man's daily actions."

"The man without such a purpose has no way to tell what is important to him. However sincere he may be at the start, he has to end up as whim-ridden, erratic, directionless, i.e., as irrational."

"There is only one purpose that can serve as the integrating standard of a man's life: productive work."

After the big build-up, the assertion that you can't do it and the threat that you'll be sorry if you try, the conclusion seems a little lame. However, as the author expands this conclusion, productive work acquires an aura of the Holy Grail. Here we have the single-minded quest which motivates all of Ayn Rand's fictional heroes and heroines except Dominique Francon, the wealthy coquette. I admire any individual with a single-minded purpose (who does not work for the state), but I would not burden my children with the expectation.

"One cannot substitute people for work." That is, one man's opinion is not the same as another man's accomplishment. That's true.

"A life of purpose is an expression of the virtue of rationality." The human potential for rational thinking now becomes a virtue, leaving us with a pious utterance of dubious meaning.

"First he must be pursuing a productive purpose. Only then, as a complement to such pursuit, is he fit for love, parties, or a social life." This has a decidedly monastic ring to it and it fits in with the generally threatening tone of the essay. This tone would be appropriate to a pre-funeral oration to the scumbags who infest what is left of Western Civilization, but it is hardly appropriate for the kind of people who will take the trouble to read this book. In this respect, the author mimics Rand's syntax very well.

The author retreats from his lofty demands in the end. "The moral issue is: how do you approach the field of work given your intellectual endowment and the existing possibilities? Are you going through the motions of holding a job, without focus or ambition, waiting for week-ends, vacations, and retirement? Or are you doing the most and the best that you can with your life? Have you committed yourself to a purpose, i.e., to a productive *career*? Have you picked a field that makes demands on you, and are you striving to meet them, to do good work, and to build on it—to expand your knowledge, develop your ability, improve your efficiency?

"If the answers to these last questions are yes, then you are totally virtuous in regard to productiveness, whether you are a surgeon or a steelworker, a house painter or a painter of landscapes, a janitor or a company president."

I am trying to imagine a janitor "with a passionate ambition for *values*." Read this essay again with a janitor in mind and see what kind of impression it makes.

"In evaluating an individual's productiveness morally, one must judge not by form or results, but by volitional essentials."

You mean to say, after all the pontificating about the principle of central purpose, productive work, that we should judge a person by his *intentions*? I prefer to judge surgeons (and janitors) by their results, thank you.

We can dispense with emotionally charged words like morals, ethics, and virtue and express the issue as Galambos did, very simply: Volitional beings live to pursue happiness and all definitions of happiness which preclude coercion are valid. Seek your happiness without coercion. No highs, no lows, no drama, no pounding the lectern, no demands, no threats, no special categories, and no contradictions, just an elegantly simple postulate that renders the syntax of Rand, Peikoff, and Objectivism redundant, unnecessary, and obsolete.

John Galt, in the context of *Atlas Shrugged*, may be justified in speaking to the masses in the tone of the Old Testament God of Wrath. For thirty years I have wondered why that syntax became the model for the voice of Objectivism. What breach of logic does that syntax serve to conceal? Individualism and political government are incompatible and the middle-class is drowning in a sea of democracy. Objectivism cannot support both the ideals of individualism and political democracy without supporting a logical contradiction. Is this, then, the source of Objectivism's emotional, archaic syntax? In our rapidly declining civilization, the need for dispassionate reason is greater than ever before. Please, leave your emotional, obscure appeals to fiction, where they belong.

# Andrew J. Galambos
# And
# The Science of Volition

**A Retrospective**

**1995**

The social and political chaos of the seventies is largely forgotten now. Certainly the baby-boomers would like to forget that decade. I suppose, in a sense, they were only acting out the irrational principles of their parents and their schools; teenagers, after all, cannot be held responsible for believing the lies they are told. The twin frauds of the war on communism and the war on poverty had catapulted the economy into double-digit inflation, the cost of living tripled in as many years; student rebellions became murderous, messianic cults flourished, cultural standards plummeted, and the political tools of force were turned against the citizens. People like me were driven to find a way to stop, or at least slow down, the collapse of our civilization. Already, by 1965, I anticipated armed troops on every street corner, checkpoints on every highway, taps on every telephone, and neighbors murdering neighbors for scraps of raw potatoes within ten years.

That scenario did not happen for several reasons. There was vast wealth in the hands of the middle-class and a strong self-interest in keeping it there. The political government backed away from its "wars" and the taxation necessary to wage them. The baby-boomers started to grow up. But a powerful, unacknowledged factor in slowing down the rate of decline was the work of Ayn Rand. If you think my statement is outrageous, remember for a moment who runs the Federal Reserve Board; Alan Greenspan was a student of Objectivism, a contributor to Ayn Rand's publications, and one of her closest friends for many years.

Galambos frequently used a quotation from Isaac Newton: "If I have seen farther than others, it is because I stood on the shoulders of giants." Ayn Rand was one such giant. Galambos did not like to admit how much in debt he was both to her thinking and to her market. Hundreds of people came to him from her market. I was one.

Let me put in a disclaimer here. I am writing about Galambos' innovations as I understood them and not necessarily as he tried to communicate them. Switching from the word "idea" to the word "innovation" is my responsibility, even though he often used the words interchangeably. In no sense can this essay be considered an exact transcription of knowledge I learned twenty years ago. Finally, my opinions are my own.

I was introduced to the Free Enterprise Institute by Dr. Richard Hunt in 1972. I attended classes throughout every year until the psychology class in the fall of 1978, which I dropped in anger during the third session. I learned some truly important things during those six years that I want to pass along.

First a little background on FEI. Andrew J. Galambos was a physicist and mathematician who started working in the aerospace industry in the fifties. Cost-plus NASA contracts caused unbelievable waste and bureaucratic inefficiency and for a young man in love with the idea of space travel, the job was pure agony. He focused his attention on the stock market and eventually bought his freedom; at the same time, he was trying to figure out what was wrong with the world and what to do about it. He began giving lectures on his ideas to small groups in 1962.

It seems kind of strange at first to sit at a table in a motel conference room with a bunch of strangers and listen to a tape recorder. However, among his introductory remarks was a statement something like this: Every civilization in the history of man on earth has collapsed; it's time we did something about it. I forgot the tape recorder, the room, the people, and the setting. I knew I had come to the right place.

The course was called V-50T, An Introduction to Volitional Science. I had only the vaguest notion of what science was about at the time since I had focused my attention on history and philosophy. Galambos gave us the epistemology of science, answering the question, how do you know for sure that what you think you know is true? What is knowledge? How do you acquire it? The scientific method answers these questions. (The epistemology of Ayn Rand's Objectivism also answers these questions.)

The scientific method consists of four steps.

1. Observation for data gathering.
2. Hypothesis formulation.
3. Extrapolation.
4. Observation for corroboration.

+Occam's Razor (for brevity)

One of the clearest examples in the history of our species involves the law of falling bodies discovered by Galileo. Throughout history people intuitively "knew" that heavy objects fall faster than light objects. Using a smooth, straight plank, Galileo rested one end on a table and the other end on the floor, then he rolled various sized balls down the plank. This is step one, observation. He determined that the popular wisdom was wrong. His hypothesis was that heavy objects and light objects fall at the same rate and that this phenomenon was a property of gravitation itself. He extrapolated to predict that this hypothesis would be true at any time and in any place. Nobody believed him. So he arranged the public demonstration at leaning tower of Pisa That was step four.

A science consists of observables. If something is not observable, then it doesn't exist. The concept of observable itself simply means brought into human sensory awareness. Electrons, for example, are not observable directly, but their existence can be brought to our awareness with instruments which are observable.

The science of volition begins with postulates; a postulate is an axiom, a starting place, a least common denominator, i.e., there is nothing more basic that is observable. There are two: 1. All volitional beings live to pursue happiness. 2. All concepts of happiness are valid which do not involve coercion. Galambos spent a lot of time investigating these postulates with the scientific method. I'm going to pass. What he was saying was that human beings live to pursue happiness and that the truth of this is an observable fact. Then he rules out coercion as a valid human method of pursuing happiness.

Coercion he defined an "any attempted, intentional interference with the property of another volitional being." And property is defined as "individual volitional being's life and any non-procreative derivatives of that life." In other words, he was saying that any pursuit of happiness is valid which does not involve interference with your life, your ideas, or your tangible possessions.

To define a durable system of social organization, Galambos' approach was to begin with a solid scientific base and then to create products derived from that base that people could freely buy; from these products would come liberty and justice and a guarantee of all of the individual human rights that mankind perennially desires and periodically loses. For the sake of consistency, I call this economic government, that is government without a coercive political state.

The revolutionary new concept that Galambos discovered and developed he called primary property, the ownership and control of ideas. Galambos knew perfectly well that some people would object to this definition, so he did not extrapolate from it in the introductory course. I had to wait until September, 1973, to take the year-long course called V-201T, which was that extrapolation. In the meantime, I took V-130T on insurance and investments and V-40T on Thomas Paine, the true author of the Declaration of Independence.

The new world which Galambos unveiled in V-201T had its roots in remodeled institutions of banking, insurance, and, at the heart of it all, what he called the clearinghouse.

When you write a check and mail it to somebody far away, it comes back to you through one or two clearing houses; that's what we mean when we say the check "cleared" the bank. The clearinghouse concept goes back to the times of caravans and bazaars where goods and money were concentrated in a central location and traded. Galambos applied the concept to primary property.

As I proceed from this point, I'm going to refer to primary property as innovations, not as ideas per se. I think that much of the confusion Galambos generated was due to the rather loose understanding people have about the word "idea" and they jumped to the conclusion that somehow they were expected to keep track of the origin of every idea they had picked up during their lifetime, an intolerable burden. The word "innovation" means "something new introduced" and it is in this sense that I use the word.

The new purpose of the clearinghouse is to act as a repository of primary property, a kind of innovation bank, if you will. Let me give you an example of how it would work.

Let's say that Microsoft releases a new word processing program, Word Ten. In a world of rational human beings, let's say one-tenth of one percent of the profit is paid to the clearinghouse as royalties to all of the innovators whose innovations were used to create Word Ten. These royalties would be weighted by time and by value, that is, recent innovations in software would be worth more. Bill Gates himself may be rated 100 (no units) in recent time, Maxwell and Faraday about 35, and Archimedes 1. In between Gates and Archimedes are thousands, if not millions, of assignments. The clearinghouse computers would do the work. As the royalties roll in, each innovator on the software tree of innovation is credited with a sum of money.

Most people won't even pay attention to it. It will be of keen interest to innovators and entrepreneurs, however, a minority in any civilization at any time. Living innovators will have control of the use of their innovations by direct contract with entrepreneurs who make things and sell them and they will retain this control after they die. Living innovators will be able to specify the use of their primary property after their death for the first time in history.

Galambos applied a simple principle to insurance, where there is risk, insure against it. Anything that you can think of as a risk ought to be insurable. Let's begin with your primordial property, your life. As I write in 1995, any living being is guaranteed to die (this may not always be the case). So we gamble that we will live in reasonably good health for so long, let's say eighty years. Within this brief time, a person may intend to accomplish certain things like acquire an education, buy a home, raise a family, achieve competence in some field, and, perhaps, create something new to mankind. During this time the person incurs the risk of dying before these goals are accomplished. The risk from accident is high during youth and early adulthood. The risk from system failures is high during the middle years. The risk from disease is high during the late years. The risk from random murder is high throughout life in our declining civilization. We should be able to insure our lives against all of these risks as they are likely to occur and in whatever amount we deem appropriate. For example, if I am forty and I am a hundred-thousand in debt and I anticipate borrowing twice that before I can market a bright new idea I've been working on, I would insure my life for three-hundred thousand. (Lenders would automatically issue life and disability insurance to any borrower; to make insurance optional on a loan is insane.) Against the risk of murder, I would insure my life for twenty-five million if I could. You will see why in a moment.

In a rational society, you would also insure your primary property, your innovations, from the risk of theft and the risk of misuse. Nicola Tesla was a brilliant innovator. At the time Thomas Edison was lighting New York City with direct current, an expensive and inefficient method of power distribution, Tesla was inventing the alternating current generator which would come to light up the whole planet. This was stolen from him. Tesla invented the florescent light. Stolen. Tesla did research on standing ground waves which nobody to this day can duplicate. As an old man in the late '30s, both broken and broke, Tesla offered the defense department a device that would destroy any enemy plane or ship two-hundred miles off shore, but he wisely refused to demonstrate it before they signed a contract with him. The newspapers called it the "Death Ray". The government refused. Tesla shrugged. And we plunged into WW II, unnecessarily, it would seem. A man like Tesla would have been first in line to buy primary property insurance. Another example is the famous conflict between Elisha Gray and Alexander Bell. They simultaneously and independently invented the telephone, but Bell beat Gray to the patent office by three hours. Gray wasted his life and his fortune seeking justice. He needed insurance. The Wright brothers had even patented ideas stolen through the duplicity of political governments; seeking justice cost Wilbur his life, Orville retired, shrugging. The list of innovators who have been victimized and exploited is as long as the list of innovators. The women and men on whose shoulders Western Civilization rests are the first, earliest, most consistent victims of coercion. The insurance company who will guarantee to protect their innovations will be very busy.

Insuring secondary property against loss would not be much different in a rational society. Insurance companies would probably take more interest in the physical condition and the whereabouts of the property than they do today. I can't see any reason to insure real estate on the Hayward fault, for example, nor would I sell fire insurance to myself, knowing what I know about the electrical wiring in this fire-trap. On the other hand, insurance would be available that is presently illegal, like insuring against loss on a venture-capital speculation, for example.

The key role and the major significance of the new insurance industry, however, is justice. The insurance company will seek to recover any loss that results from coercion. Thus, if I am murdered, my killer will face restitution of my life insurance. Of course, my killer may have insured himself against this risk. The clearinghouse will also set a penalty against the man which he cannot erase for all time. But let's say the killer does not have insurance and let's say he does not care about his reputation in future generations. Does he walk away free? Yes and no. There is no institution of coercion to force my killer to do anything, yet there is no reason why the business community in this rational society should want to do business with him. The insurance company informs the banks and the banks suspend the man's debit cards. Suddenly, my killer cannot use the transportation and communication systems; suddenly, his residential infrastructure is turned off; suddenly, he cannot even buy a candy bar from a vending machine. In other words, my killer either pays for his crime, literally, or he starves.

This concept of justice is elegantly simple. Any person who interferes with another person's property, pays for it, period. The price is fixed by the person who owns the property with the insurance she buys to protect her property. The insurance company pays the claim, then collects the debt which the criminal has incurred. The criminal either covers his debt with insurance of his own or pays with his assets or makes arrangements to pay. A refusal to cooperate guarantees the criminal two options, starvation or expulsion from society.

I would like to reiterate that no individual is compelled to buy insurance in this rational society; there are NO institutions of coercion in a rational society. Insurance would seem to be in any individual's rational self-interest, however, to protect her property from risk of loss. Beware the temptation to compare insurance premiums with taxation; you have no choice to pay taxes, it's your money or your life. Also beware the temptation to compare insurance premiums of the future with insurance premiums of the present; in a rational society, the risks to property will be minimal, i.e., there will be powerful proprietary interest in making risks minimal. Now let us turn to the banking industry.

Many of the hardware innovations which Galambos described in the seventies have subsequently come into existence, including the debit card, the automatic teller, and paypoint. Unfortunately the banks have not yet recognized the true value of paypoint and they penalize the customer by charging for use of the debit card. This system could easily replace paper and coin money; when it does, you will find a crucial tool of the new justice system in place: a criminal's debit card won't work. (The PIN system is risky, however, and needs to be replaced.) Another security measure in place is the electronic investigation of an account applicant's banking history; a bad-check writer cannot open a new account.

The heart of any banking system, of any economy, is money. The call for a return to the gold standard is founded on the absolute nature of the metal, so absolute, in fact, that our political government got rid of its gold. The dollar itself now rests on our political government's power to tax and power to print and power to manipulate the banking industry. As our middle-class begins to drown in the flood of new taxes coming to support our socialist economy in the next century, however, the political government will neither be able meet its bond obligations nor fund its socialist programs; inflation and even higher taxation will result. The Russian economy of today is an instructive model to study.

The banking system, the whole financial structure, in fact, was to be based on primary property. Galambos' vision of man was that of an intergalactic species and his vision of time was measured in millennia, therefore no basis of wealth limited to earth would be adequate. Primary property, however, could be expected to be universal among rational species who had advanced beyond the coercive political stage. The clearinghouse would quickly become a reservoir of vast wealth, the permanent and durable savings account of civilization, and would generate an ever increasing prosperity throughout the civilization. Like innovation itself, the wealth can expand forever; as with innovation itself, inflation is impossible. Inflation only occurs with the destruction of wealth, as in riots or wars or coercive welfare, or the introduction of more money for a fixed number of goods, as in coercive managed economies, i.e., wage-price freezes, or "Five-year Plans." Innovation and wealth go hand in hand, both can expand indefinitely. Innovation and wealth can only be curtailed by coercion and the mechanism in both cases is the same, armed robbery.

The number one question at this point is, how do we establish the institutions of the clearinghouse, insurance, and banking inside of a coercive political state? What will serve as a bridge between this civilization and the next? Galambos seemed to believe that the proliferation of his innovations was, in fact, that bridge. From where I sit twenty odd years later, I think he was wrong. He wanted to keep a handle on his innovations, which is understandable, but I never heard a concrete description of the bridge mechanism. I recall three models of imaginary scenarios, however, which served as examples of how things might work. One was in a spaceship, naturally. Now that the government's space program is bankrupt, a proprietary space program is a remote possibility; all that is lacking is the right entrepreneur with the right innovations. The second model was a proprietary, enclosed city built somewhere on the great plains. I believe that idea has a better chance in the near-term future given, again, the right entrepreneur with the right innovations. If one could circumvent the state long enough to get it off the ground, then the problem would be defending it against the IRS in conjunction with the military; attracting that much capital investment would also attract the looters who run this country. The third model was a proprietary ocean-traveling ship, a self-contained, mobile city of working entrepreneurs and innovators; the problems inherent in this model are obvious.

For years I have predicted the collapse of our socialist economy when the baby-boomers reach the age of sixty-five between 2012 and 2030. Any pyramid racket collapses when it exhausts its base and the number of taxpayers is not growing. As the numbers decline further and the demand for socialist services grows, the American middle-class will be impoverished by taxation. The only hope of a near-term solution that I can see is to find some way for the middle-class to hide its wealth from the political state. We must find a way to send our money to banks located in off-shore tax havens without the IRS knowing about it. A large enough financial reserve, which would be no secret, by the way, only the specific individual's identity would be secret, would keep world economies afloat during the coming crisis and would prevent a headlong rush into another Dark Age, from which, I'm afraid, our species would never again emerge. As the political government fails during this crisis, the opportunity to establish the institutions of economic government will rise. Again, a reserve of wealth which cannot be stolen would serve to accelerate the transition.

I will not live long enough to find out what happens. My children will take the most punishment from the economic crisis during the second and third decades of the next century. My grandchildren may not survive at all. To quote Mr. Galambos, "What will be the human population on this planet in a hundred years? Either very large, or zero."

(Author's note: V-50T: An Introduction to the Science of Volition was transcribed from tape and published as Volume One of *Sic Itur ad Astra* in 1999.)

# RAND vs GALAMBOS
# THE CONTRADICTIONS

## 1995

I am writing in response to an article in *The Objectivist Newsletter*, Vol.3 No.5, May, 1964, Intellectual Ammunition Department, answering the question, "What is the Objectivist position in regard to patents and copyrights?"

This was Ayn Rand's challenge to Galambos' position on ideas; he was lecturing at this time in Los Angeles in direct competition with the Nathaniel Branden Institute and Rand herself. Galambos is the only man on earth who ever suggested the permanent ownership of intellectual property; without Galambos, the subject did not exist, yet Rand never mentions his name. This is the first of several statements she made on the issue over the years; as far as I know, the mistakes contained in this essay were consistently repeated.

Beginning with the question itself, Rand confines the topic to existing legal tools of political government. She does not want to deal with the question outside of this context, yet the question of ownership of ideas is an existing fact of reality which precedes, and creates the demand for, any institutional tool that deals with it. The evasion of this fact is her first error. Ownership of innovation, after ownership of one's life, is the foundation of all property rights. In the context of *Atlas Shrugged*, Rand says the same thing. Here, she insists on the existing legal context which makes the proposition absurd.

After making an obvious distinction between physical and intellectual, she gets back to the point, "the origination of an *idea*," in the continuing context of political law. Paragraph three: "An idea as such cannot be protected until it has been given material form." Is that true? In the sense that an idea is a collection of electro-chemical processes residing in an individual human brain, it is transparently true. But we are not trying to protect an idea as such, we are trying to protect the "origination" of an idea, the issue she immediately returns to. But first, she writes, "An invention has to be embodied in a physical model...; a story has to be written or printed." Why?

The question is, does any form of disclosure establish ownership? Here, Rand says, no, ownership is only established by registration with the government. Galambos answers, yes, verbal disclosure establishes ownership. I cannot imagine that Rand disagreed with this privately in regard to her own ideas, she epitomized her own concept of rational self-interest, and in light of everything she had written on the subjects of innovation and contracts up to this point, her position is a blatant contradiction of her own principles.

In paragraph four, Rand distinguishes between *discovery* and *invention*. The path to discovery may be strewn with invention, as seen when Newton invented the calculus to discover the natural laws of gravitation, but she is right to draw a line between them. A discovery is an act which presumes that something exists in nature which mankind has not yet found or identified; discovery is the act of finding it. Rand asserts that a discovery cannot be patented and in that narrow legal context, she is right. That does not mean a discovery cannot be owned, however, which is what she clearly implies. She avoids the concrete analogy to a gold deposit, a material discovery which has a long tradition of ownership, and goes straight to scientific discovery. Scientists are notoriously possessive about their discoveries, rightly so, which have never been protected by any political mechanism. Rand asserts that a "discovery...cannot be the exclusive property of the discoverer" for two reasons: "(a) he did not *create* it, and (b)... he cannot demand that men continue to pursue or practice falsehoods except by his permission."

Of course he didn't create it. By definition, a discovery is a finding of preexisting facts; a prospector does not create a gold deposit, he finds it, but that does not mean he cannot own it. Her second objection means that a discovery belongs to anyone who cares to use it. I don't think the miner would agree. I don't think a scientist would agree either. If the scientists who discovered the inner workings of the atom had had an existing institution that promised to keep their discoveries out of the hands of men like Harry Truman, I think they would have turned to it for protection. The legal institutions of copyright and patent cannot cope with ownership of discovery; it is the conceptual limitation of the institutions which is inadequate, not the market demand for protection. So, let's create an institution which will fulfill the demand and let's stop calling the demand impossible.

This is precisely the issue Galambos addressed: to guarantee to innovators and discoverers ownership of their intellectual property and, thereby, control of the present and future applications of their property. Rand insisted it could not be done. Galambos showed us how to do it.

"The right to intellectual property cannot be exercised in perpetuity." This assertion in paragraph six is supported by the argument in paragraph eight: "it would lead...to the unearned support of parasitism."

It is not a "right" which is at stake here; ownership is at stake and ownership is not a right, ownership is a fact of nature. Do I own my innovation or don't I? I am not asking this of the political state, I am asking this of nature. I own my life, I own my ideas, and I own my actions in nature regardless of the political state's current spin on the question. I own my innovation when I am alive and I continue to own my innovation after I am dead regardless of the political state's, or anybody else's, current spin on the question. This is not a matter of opinion, it is a matter of fact. In the context of her own avowed specialty at the time, philosophy, Rand agrees, but in her competition with Galambos, she disagrees, elsewhere begging the question by calling it an issue belonging to the "philosophy of law", an oxymoron.

Introducing parasitism, she attacks his idea in the context of legal inheritance. If that which she says cannot be done could be done, then royalties based on the perpetual ownership of innovation would corrupt the heirs and would eventually bring innovation itself to a halt. As the innovator, however, I control what I own and I designate the use to which any wealth generated is put, that is, I don't leave it to my heirs. Again, what she claims cannot be done, Galambos showed us how to do with his clearinghouse concept.

On royalties, Rand raises the common questions of who pays how much and how can a person keep track? Only end product producers pay royalties, how much the royalties are depends on measurable factors, including remoteness in time, and the same computers that distribute royalties keep track of them. Obviously, I am talking about another new institution in business to do this kind of work. If this institution had existed, I very much doubt if Rand would have surrendered her owner- ship of her own ideas to any living person or heirs. Her rejection of the ownership of ideas is a denial of her own Law of Identity and an accept- ance of socialism, the socialism of the public library, which represents a fundamental contradiction of her position on capitalism.

The final six paragraphs of Rand's essay demonstrate the absurdity of mixing Galambos' innovations with existing political institutions, while at the same time condemning the operation of those very institutions.

I believe that Rand's purpose was to undermine Galambos' Los Angeles market. The two of them were well enough acquainted for Galambos to offer to produce a movie of *Atlas Shrugged* and for Rand to turn him down. She was indisputably the spiritual leader of the liber- tarian/capitalist movements of the time and her imprimatur had serious influence in Southern California communities. She did not approve of Galambos.

She had deeper problems. She made no attempt to reconcile the contradiction between her flag-waving American patriotism and her condemnation of political democracy. She permitted the popular delusion that the Declaration of Independence and the Constitution were expressions of the same intent to stand, while knowing perfectly well that these two documents are diametrically opposed. She insisted that economics derived from politics without ever defining what she meant by politics and without ever demonstrating the logical necessity for what appears to me an inverted proposition.

These contradictions culminate in the conclusion to *Atlas Shrugged*. While the innovators bask in Atlantis and the politicians commit suicide in Washington, the economy and the society revert to the Dark Ages. John Galt makes the sign of the dollar over the devastated country and says it's nearly time to go back. Go back to what? How are these innovators and entrepreneurs going to jump-start this dead world? She didn't say.

Ayn Rand demonstrated that mankind can no longer survive without rationality. She demonstrated that capitalism is the only economic system that works. But she could not, or refused to, invent human institutions of justice and of security to replace the failing institutions that we all know so well. Did she really believe the masses would vote themselves *out* of socialism? Her following was and is large and influential, but they number a pitiful minority compared with an electorate who believes they stand to gain more than they stand to loose by voting for socialist politicians.

Galambos approached the problem of government from a scientific point of view, not a romantic point of view, and he pointed to concrete models of human institutions that could provide security and justice without coercion. He explained why it would work and how it would work. It's a shame that Rand didn't listen to him.

# December 25: Newton Day

**1997**

**This essay is written with gratitude to the ideas of**

**Andrew J. Galambos and Simon Buckingham**

This day we celebrate the birth of the man who stood on the frontier a revolution that changed the human environment. His discoveries enabled our world of electricity, electronic communications, light, heat, medical science, industry, and transportation. Every branch of innovation since 1665 derives from this man.

He, himself, said, "If I have seen farther than others, it is because I stood on the shoulders of giants." He was not being humble; he knew perfectly well that he was one of those giants. Some of the men he called giants were Copernicus, Brahe, Kepler, Galileo, and Bruno. Not surprisingly, they were near-contemporaries.

There was another time in human history when a small number of innovators lived and worked in the same generation. Euclid, Aristarchus, and Archimedes, to mention only three, lived and worked at the same time.

In the third century before Christ, therefore, certain knowledge was available to mankind from these innovators, including the size of the earth, the distance from the sun, the place of the earth in our solar system, how our solar system worked, and the nature of the sun, i.e., that it was a star. In addition, there was algebra, geometry, and, most probably, calculus. The time was ripe for a Greek Newton.

In other words, in the third century before Christ, mankind had the same knowledge available that was made available again in the seventeenth century after Christ. By the time Jesus was born, they should have been living with electricity, automobiles, space-craft, and open-heart surgery. Why weren't they?

Because they were stuck in the political paradigm of Kings, which would not be supplanted until Thomas Paine, and they were stuck in the economic paradigm of slavery. The water-clocks and steam-engines of the Third Century B.C. were the playthings of Kings. Not one person saw the connection between the steam-engine and Archimedes screw, which would have precipitated an Agricultural Revolution and an Industrial Revolution within two-hundred years. Why should they? They had an unlimited supply of flesh and bone to do the work of their primitive civilization, as some countries still do today.

We have traded Kings, one-man rule, for committees, majority rule. This worked for a while, but it will not work in an increasingly unorganized™ world of instant communication and concomitant proliferation of self-interest and self-responsibility. People will no longer want their individual decisions made for them.

We have traded the economics of slavery for the economics of machinery, which is still limping along within the paradigm of committees trying to run it. Once again, communication and self-interest, technological-capitalism™, will unorganize this paradigm and drive the committees out and we will evolve an economic paradigm in which individuals are in charge of their own destiny.

We stand today, as Newton did in his day, on the frontier of another revolution, another turning-around, to the paradigm of economic government, a paradigm which has no kings, no committees, and no organizations, a paradigm which can pay fitting gratitude to the giants who created it. Thank you, Isaac Newton.

Addendum: Lest you conclude that I belittle Christmas by calling it Newton Day, please know that peace-on-Earth and good-will toward mankind are my own founding principles. History speaks for itself.

Note: The concepts of Unorganization™ and Technological-Capitalism™ are the property of Simon Buckingham http://www.unorg.com and used by permission.

# On Money

## 2000

This is what I understand about money: Money is any medium of exchange which is mutually acceptable to any partners involved in an exchange of property; property consists of an individual's life, material possessions, and ideas. From observation of natural law I exclude an individual's life from any exchange of property, i.e., an individual life is owned by the individual and that ownership cannot be exchanged. There is good money and there is bad money. Good money retains its relative value with respect to material possessions and ideas over time; bad money loses its relative value with respect to material possessions and ideas over time. In the absence of coercion, good money will replace bad money.

I also view money as a derivative of an individual's life. Human beings engage in activities to earn money; individuals decide to devote a certain amount of time in their limited life-time to earning money that they can exchange for goods and services as they wish. Thus there is an investing of life in money which we can examine.

For example, it is said by some that the average American wage-earner spends up to half a work-year paying taxes http://www.fraserin-stitute.ca/ptfd_disclaimer.html. If that is true, it means that half of a average wage-earner's work-life is stolen and cannot be invested as the wage-earner chooses. Is this slavery? Whatever it is called, this kind of statistic focuses attention on other questions: where does money come from, what is it worth, and who controls it?

Economists and historians tell us that money evolved from barter or trade of goods, things, commodities, moving over time from perishable things like clay pots and stone tools to more durable things like copper, silver, and gold. Gold eventually became the standard for money and it's relative value for exchange was determined by its absolute weight in a given trade. The Industrial Revolution introduced a new demand for money which made gold itself impractical due to its bulk, weight, and limited supply, so paper certificates or bearer bonds which promised an equivalent redemption value in gold began circulating. Privately owned banks became the repositories for the gold and the banks issued the paper money. Banks also took over the risky, formerly underground, business of loaning money to individuals, businesses, and governments at interest. A given bank might own gold and silver in reserve and store deposits of gold owned by others, plus own partial shares in any number of enterprises in a community, the value of which was measured in terms of gold, plus own shares in the government as bonds, which were also valued in terms of gold and silver. A bank could easily invest more money than it possessed in gold and silver reserves and if a bank's investments in enterprises and/or governments failed, the bank could fail, which was financially damaging to everybody involved. This was an insurable risk, by the way, and it is not clear to me why insurance companies did not enter this business during the Nineteenth Century, but the fact remains that a federal, central bank was finally established after a century of controversy and popular objection, in part, to solve the problem of local bank failures. (That this led to the biggest bank failures in recent history is not my subject here.) In the U.S., this central bank issued gold and silver certificates as paper money based on federal deposits of the metals held in the legendary

Fort Knox. The demand for money eventually exceeded any reasonable expectation of redemption in gold and silver, especially during times of war when money was turned into munitions and literally blown up, so the gold-standard for money was terminated. (What happened to the gold and silver in Fort Knox is also not my subject here.) The central bank today issues notes based on promises, decrees, and enforced laws. This is called fiat money, it is our money. Or is it?

I believe that we, mankind, have arrived at an unanticipated watershed in our generally accepted understanding about money and I believe a new paradigm for money is at hand. The deeply ingrained notion that there is a limited amount of money for everybody to share or exchange has been a long time dying and the observable fact that money is everyday being created is largely unrecognized, although it is true. That is to say, not all money comes from the central bank.

Consider this typical Silicon Valley scenario. A software engineer sees an unsolved problem in some application and she tries to solve it. This leads her to an altogether different idea for a new application. As she writes specifications for the new application, she realizes that this could mean a whole new business. She writes a business plan, then meets with venture capital companies to acquire start-up money. She starts a new business, she is successful, and she eventually expands into a new company with the sale of publicly offered stock.

Where does her start-up money come from? Venture capital companies are not banks, they are publicly owned stock companies, so her start-up money comes from investments made by stockholders, i.e., from the after-tax disposable income of a variety of people who are willing to risk their money on new ventures. Her start-up company creates and produces a new software product which sells and pays her costs and earns a profit for her and her venture capitalists. Where did this money come from? From the after-tax disposable incomes of the people who bought her product. She decides to expand her company to create more new products, so she sells stock to raise the necessary money. Where does that money come from? From the after-tax disposable incomes of people willing to take a risk on her stock in anticipation of future profits.

Because we count our money in dollars and cents, it is impossible to accurately distinguish between dollars printed and gratuitously poured into the economy by the government's central bank and dollars created in the marketplace by innovators and entrepreneurs by the creation, manufacture, and sale of new products, but the fact remains that new money is created in the marketplace which has no connection with the central bank. What is it worth?

Money is worth what it will buy, there is no absolute standard of value for money. We must not forget here that money includes the lifetime investment of the individual. Governments' adventures in war and market manipulations have time and time again devalued fiat money until, at some points in recent history, it took a bushel of paper money to buy a potato (I wonder how much life-time it took to acquire the bushel of paper, that was the real value of the money). American people have a distinct advantage in our year 2000 because money is being created faster than it is being destroyed and we consequently have enough after-tax money to freely buy from a plentiful market of goods and services. The very existence of this abundance and the uncountable millions of money transactions which occur every day stabilize the value of money against the destruction of money by political governments (curiously, there might even be a kind of balance between money governments print and money governments destroy, though there is no accounting of this in terms of money or life-time wasted on it.)

Who controls money? From the stern edicts of government to the knee-jerk reactions of stock markets, it appears that the American people may believe that the Federal Reserve controls money in their political jurisdiction. I don't, although I did. I think that the Federal Reserve and the powers-that-be behind it have been gradually losing control of money since the end of our Viet Nam debacle and the double-digit inflation it spawned. I think that this is the result of the gradually increasing creation of new money in the marketplace. I think that the control of this new money is largely in the hands of the people, not the government, thus far.

The new money today is still called dollars, but it is seldom represented by Federal Reserve Notes any more. Most of the new money exists and is exchanged as strings and rows of zeros and ones, digital cash, or ecash. The creation and rapid proliferation of ecash has alarmed some people, even some who should know better. About a month ago I came across a serious, though perhaps misinformed, objection to ecash written by an economist. To me this essay represents a clash of paradigms, the old paradigm for money as paper issued by and controlled by political governments, and the new paradigm for money as ecash created in the marketplace and controlled by ordinary people in the marketplace. I would like to briefly explore the similarities and the differences in these paradigms to see what the future may hold in store for us. I quote from the essay by Professor Frank Shostak, chief economist at Ord-Minnett, Australia, entitled *The Electronic Money Myth*, which was published at <http://www.lewrockwell.com> on June 23, 2000. Professor Shostak begins (I put his words in *italics*):

*Many economists and financial commentators believe that in the unregulated market of the internet economy, new forms of money can be created that bypass central-bank and government supervision. The latest development is the emergence of a new electronic means of payment. Experts maintain it will displace the existent fiat money. This displacement will usher in a new era of free banking, it is claimed, where competition between banks' electronic moneys will finally put to rest the menace of inflation.*

*Unfortunately, this is a pipe dream. Electronic money will not replace fiat paper money. The belief that it can stems from a failure to understand the nature and function of money and how it emerges on the market.*

*Electronic money, or digital money, takes the form of a "smart" card, containing a microchip that the user pre-programs with a specific dollar amount [See David Friedman and Kerry Lynn Macintosh "Technology and the Case for Free Banking" unpublished paper]. To make a purchase, the card is swiped through a special card reader, which automatically deducts the amount of the purchase from the stored value on the card and credits the amount to seller's account.*

Professor Shostak's use of the term "free banking" is interesting in his introduction. I presume that he means regulation-free and I think he might do well to listen to what the "experts" are saying.

The professor's example of a "pipe dream" is unfortunate. The "smart card" is only one way proposed to carry and to transfer electronic money and, as far as I know at the moment, does not exist. A "debit card" works very well to transfer ecash from one's personal bank account to a merchant's bank account; I buy groceries and gasoline and pay monthly bills with a debit card. The bank itself may be a brick and mortar building on a street corner or it may exist solely on-line. I can also transfer money on the Internet via PayPal and E-Gold to buy what I wish and competing methods of transferring money on-line are being developed everywhere.

*Furthermore, money must emerge as a commodity. An object cannot be used as money unless it already possesses an objective exchange value based on some other use. The object must have a pre-existing price for it to be accepted as money.*

Ecash is not an object and is not a commodity, ecash consists of electronic digits, strings and rows of zeros and ones. Fiat money is an object and is a commodity, printed paper and stamped metal are both material objects and commodities. However, neither ecash nor fiat money possess "an objective exchange value based on some other use." True, paper and brass have a market value as commodities, both do have some other use and electronic zeros and ones do not, but that value is subjective, not objective; commodities are only worth as much as people are willing to pay for them. A piece of paper with a hundred-dollars printed on it has no more exchange value as money than a string of electronic digits signifying a hundred-dollars. The exchange value of fiat money and of ecash is relative and subjective and is based only on the millions of common, everyday transactions in world markets, including my local supermarket; neither have a "pre-existing price" and both are accepted as money.

*The benefit money offers is its purchasing power, i.e. its price in terms of goods and services. Consequently for something to be accepted as money, it must have a pre-existing purchasing power: a price. This price could have only emerged if it had an exchange value established in barter.*

Ecash is also only worth as much as it will buy, that is exactly what it is worth, but it does not come with "a pre-existing purchasing power" any more than babies come with a pre-existing PhD. This repetition sounds like dogma to me. True, gold and paper are commodities that have a market value, though not an equal value by weight, but neither have a "pre-existing purchasing power" either. A piece of paper with a hundred-dollars printed on it will buy a hundred-dollars worth of the same stuff as ecash, their relative purchasing power is the same.

*The fact that an object must have a pre-exiting price before it becomes money precludes the possibility that money in a free market could be issued by just anybody. In fact, the idea that anybody can print his own money, and for that money to be accepted in exchange, is preposterous. Why would anyone accept notes printed by Mr Jones or even by a famous movie star? This possibility, however, is implied by the view which endorses the issuance of electronic money based on paper notes issued by banks or private entrepreneurs.*

Ecash is not about "issuing" money, ecash is about creating money. The professor would like us to regard ecash as an economist might have regarded bearer bonds or notes issued by a private bank in 1816, a Jones Dollar or something like that. An ecash dollar is still a dollar, the questions are where did it come from and who controls it?

*Moreover, the whole idea that electronic money could somehow replace fiat money is not defendable. Electronic money can function only as long as individuals know that they can convert it into fiat money, i.e. cash on demand (see, e.g., Lawrence H. White "The Technology Revolution And Monetary Evolution," Cato Institute's 14th annual monetary conference, May 23, 1996).*

People managed to function with fiat paper money after their gold and silver certificates were declared worthless, so I cannot accept the professor's claim of necessity here. I imagine that fiat paper dollars will coexist with ecash dollars comfortably until one form of dollar becomes more desirable than the other, in the absence of armed force, that is.

*Because electronic money is not real money but merely a different way of employing existent fiat money obviously, it cannot replace it.*

Ecash "is a new way of employing" money, but not "existent" money, ecash is a new way of employing emergent money. Political governments regulate their money supply in several ways, one of which is issuing a finite quantity of paper and coin printed with a money exchange value. This finite quantity of money cannot and does not account for or limit the emergence and growth of real monetary values in the marketplace which are a direct result of uninhibited and unanticipated innovation. New markets are created that our political government masters and their servants never imagined and new wealth is created in its wake. The only action political government can take to control emergent wealth is to steal it or to destroy the source of it. Most of this new wealth, if not all, is created, circulated, and exchanged as ecash.

*In their recent paper David Friedman and Kerry Macintosh argue that the new technology would make it possible to implement sophisticated barter. This in turn would completely remove the need for money ("Technology and the case for free banking," unpublished paper).*

*However, why should the essence of barter be altered on account of a new technology? How could a professor of economics make his living if food producers were not interested in directly exchanging their goods for lectures in economics? This new technology does not resolve this issue, any more than technology alone can create a new form of money to replace existing fiat moneys. For the duration, or until we have serious efforts at far-reaching monetary reform, the most new technology can offer is new forms of efficiency in payment and record keeping. But it will not alter the essence of money itself.*

I daresay the professor is correct in doubting a trade of lectures for food and I also believe that money is here to stay, however it is his remark about "far-reaching monetary reform" that catches my attention. Reform by whom? What is he talking about? Reform in thinking by academic economists? Reform by political governments and their central banks? Must we have a decree to acknowledge what is happening? Monetary reform is already underway and it is not being done by public servants, academicians, or think tanks, it is being done by a host of unknown innovators and entrepreneurs across the planet who would like to have a stable, realistic monetary system in place, available to the common human being whose life-time is at stake and unavailable to their political states. Ecash can and will accomplish what the gold-standard and fiat money could not accomplish: liberty and justice for individuals everywhere. That could be our future.

# Problems With Paradigms

## 2000

Paradigm: an example serving as a model. Somehow this simple concept has a way of slipping into obscurity, if not meaninglessness, when it is applied to the concept of government. I'm not sure why. Perhaps it is because we already have a deeply entrenched understanding of government as a set of rules to regulate behavior and as a body of rulers who create and enforce the rules. The little we know about the history of mankind would seem to support this explanation; how often has it been said that history consists of warfare? And what is warfare but governments enforcing their rules? So do we think of government as a lofty group of rule-makers backed up by armies of killers? I believe we do harbor some such notion. But does this concept of government cover the entire subject in everyday reality? No, I don't think it does, I think it represents only one paradigm or model for government, a paradigm of force or coercion, which I call political government.

My choice of words here is not accidental, there really is another model or paradigm for government in operation in everyday life and the history of mankind is rich with stories and incidents along the course of its development. Modern historians call it commerce.

Commerce: an exchange of goods and services. This limited definition seems to preclude any concept of government and we get the picture of half-naked pastoral nomads trading seashells for stone tools, which may indeed be where it all began, though the image is hardly relevant today. When I think of commerce, I think of twenty-acre enclosed and air-conditioned shopping malls and miles of freight trucks and ships and aircraft bringing in goods from manufacturers all over the planet; I think of whole city blocks of health-care providers' offices and of hospitals equipped with millions of dollars worth of equipment to diagnose and to treat human illnesses; I think of The Yellow Pages listing thousands of individuals and groups who offer goods and services for sale; I think of the Internet. This is commerce. Is it also government?

Govern: To rule by right of authority; to exercise a directing influence; to control. Is the concept of governing applicable to commerce? Let's say that I have an idea for a new product that I want to manufacture, distribute, and sell to the public. To keep this simple, let's also say that I already have a lot of money and that I'm kind of shy and I don't know how to organize a company. First, I will contract with somebody who does know how to organize a company and I will give that person the authority to get the job done. Then I'll stay home and tinker with another new idea. Let's say that eventually there are several thousand people engaged in manufacturing, distributing, and selling my products. Did this all happen by some kind of mysterious spontaneous generation? Or did it happen by deliberate and careful direction of activity? Was it governed activity? I think there is little room to quibble about the meaning of words here. Corporations are governments. But corporations do not require the use of force to accomplish their purpose, so corporations are not political governments. I call this form of human organization economic government.

I could have called it something else, like voluntary or cooperative government, but I think that mixes the concept up with democracy, which is another form of political or coercive government. A term like corporate government is also confusing because it is already used in the sense of corporate structure or hierarchy and it leaves out the important concept of a one-person business. Economics, however, is fundamental to commerce; one could even say that economics is the brainchild of commerce, an intellectual interpretation of human activity which already exists. Commercial government might be a useful term, though it sounds to me like coercive political government for sale, which some may say also already exists. In the end, I picked a term that doesn't exist in some other context, economic government, to refer to a model or paradigm of human activity which is private, individual, voluntary, contractual, and commercial and which totally leaves out force or fraud, coercion that is, as a method of operation.

Unfortunately, identifying a new model or paradigm for government does not solve the problem of paradigms. People will continue to view events within the paradigm that they learned as children and presume that it is the only way to view events. I find that viewing events through the lens of paradigms to be very useful, however. Political government cannot create wealth, for example, it can only steal it or destroy it, while economic government is all about creating wealth—stealing it is unnecessary and counterproductive, and destroying it is insane. People with the best of intentions in the paradigm of political government must always resort to the use of force to carry out their intentions, along with the fraud that their ends justify their means, while in economic government the use of force is unnecessary and counterproductive because it destroys wealth, which is insane. To be very effective at lying, cheating, and stealing will get a person ahead in political government, while these activities in economic government are a sure-fire way to lose personal reputation and market-share and to guarantee failure.

It takes time for paradigms to change. Not so long ago the prevailing paradigm for political government was monarchial, then Thomas Paine came along and dethroned the Kings, though the idea continues to persist amongst various chairpersons and presidents. Some would like to modify the paradigm of political government to pull its teeth, as it were, to curtail its use of coercion. But political government is coercive government, there is no way to modify that. I do think that over time certain services we've come to expect from political government, like security and justice, will shift toward economic government simply because people want it and it will be cheaper and it will work—we're seeing this kind of shift in shopping malls already—and then I imagine the paradigm for government itself will begin to change.

# Enlightenment

## 2001

I would like to repeat a story that I heard sometime, somewhere, that was probably invented by somebody else, elsewhere; I take it for fiction. A lady comes up to Einstein and asks him what the theory of relativity means for religion and he replies, it doesn't mean anything, they are two different subjects.

Yes, well, that was a polite and perhaps an appropriate answer, but we know it wasn't quite true. Relativity and its brainchild, quantum physics, have had a profound effect on our understanding of God.

Natural human curiosity and the advancements made in scientific technology have enabled our species to see inside the invisible forces of energy that make up reality as our gross senses know it and there we discovered an inconceivable and nearly indescribable new reality of energy. Energy comes in strange packages; these are not things or objects familiar to our senses. Energy is charged, energy spins, energy pops into existence and pops out of existence, energy affects energy instantaneously at a distance. Energy breaks all of our old rules. What does it mean to us?

We are made of energy, the Earth is made of energy, the Universe is made of energy. We consume energy, our life burns energy, we exchange energy, we excrete energy. What is consciousness? Is it energy? How could it not be energy? Does something exist that is not energy? I don't think so.

Granted, when I believe that consciousness is energy I am making a leap of faith from the context of physics to the context of psychology. I make a further leap of faith in my belief that the universe of energy is also the universe of consciousness, that they are one and the same. I make the final leap of faith in my belief that the universe of consciousness is God. From that I extrapolate that the universe we can observe with our senses and our instruments is the manifestation of God. We, the living, are brief manifestations of consciousness, which is energy, which is God, and we can choose to connect our intelligence to that universal consciousness if we want to, even though we don't have the sensory equipment or the technology to prove it. Yet.

My assertions and my beliefs are nothing new, people have been saying more or less the same thing for thousands of years. The verbal stories and the written stories from the past are rich in varied imagery that attempts to describe what is essentially a non-sensory, non-verbal experience common to all people at all times. Religions were founded on this kind of imagery, but the vision of the founders was always usurped by materially ambitious people who turned it into a codified prescription for enslavement, that is into political government. Organized religions are no more and no less political governments than the military-industrial-congressional states that rule us in the secular world today; in the Middle-East, of course, they are usually identical. I cannot think of a greater perversion of human capability than to take the message in the image of "Love thy neighbor as thyself," and twist it into "Kill thy neighbor for your religious state."

For the record, let me put this plainly, I am not an atheist; I believe in God. I also believe that one day we will be able to prove the existence of God as the origin of the universe as energy as consciousness with scientific instruments and that we will verify that individual human beings can willfully touch minds with God and with each other without help from an intermediary.

Some say that the belief in God is irrational. I say that the denial of observational reality is irrational. When we discover observational data that does not fit our hypothesis, then we had better alter our hypothesis, not ignore the data. What will this mean for religion? Why, not a thing, they are two different subjects.

# Writing

## 2001

Writing is a seductive activity. Here there are few rules to obey and limitless vistas to explore without ever leaving the comfort and the amenities of one's home. One can engage in riot or fight old battles again without speaking a word. One can carry out a love affair between strangers and enjoy their pleasures and feel their pain without paying the price for either. Writing is better than reading because the writer is in charge of the story and the writer can take it whither he pleases. The writer can make it rain on a sunny day or make it hot when it's cold and nature cannot contradict him.

There are writers who invent horrible scenes of suffering, of fear, and of failure. I wonder about these writers, I wonder about their state of mind when they invent these scenes. I wonder if they really perceive life through a malevolent lens or if they are only meditating on the unpleasant horrors of our recent history, like throwing live babies into prison-camp furnaces. When horrors become commonplace acts, I suppose there is no limit to horrors imaginable.

I have a problem with that sort of imagination myself. Although I know what evil mankind is capable of doing—the Germans and the Russians of the Twentieth Century were no different in this regard than the Mongols and the Vikings of the Tenth—I can find no good reason to celebrate it anew in my writing. Destruction is not the same as creation and I choose to celebrate creation.

Writing itself can be creative or destructive depending on the accuracy of perception and the honesty of the writer. Lies are easy to spread; some lies are even taken for truth, such as the popular lies about the need for political government. Writers who contribute to such fairy tales do mankind a disservice; the nation-state has proved to be the most destructive social institution mankind ever invented and we have centuries of evidence to prove it. Communicating a positive new vision of human social organization that could provide security and justice without the use of force or fraud would be truly creative writing.

Autobiographical writing can be useful in evaporating myths about the writer or in creating new ones. Again, it's a question of perception and honesty. People in general seem to enjoy talking about themselves; some talk about little else. I am fond of reading what some writers have to say about themselves, Thoreau, for example, but I shy away from writers who insist on describing their misery. In a sense, anything that anybody writes is autobiographical in that it involves personal choices of subject and syntax, although skilled writers can convey an impression of themselves that is entirely false. Thus I may write an essay that is aggressive, judgmental, and offensive when in real life I am passive, forgiving, and pleasant—or vice versa. What is the truth?

I must confess that sometimes I lose track of the truth in the elegance of the written word. It is fairly easy to take such facts as one knows about and then to spin a clever tale around them, perhaps condemning the innocent and exonerating the guilty in the process. We see this happen with great care and deliberation in the media as well as in the courts and in the legislatures of the land. For myself, if the subject is worthy of the effort, I will come at it from several directions to get at the truth. For others, whether the subject is worthy or not, a premeditated outcome is the object to achieve and the truth be damned; this is the essence of advertising, law, and propaganda. Polemics are juvenile. Like the use of force, this kind of fraud—information abuse—will gradually disappear as our species grows up—if there is time for that.

Andrew J. Galambos once pointed out that literacy is crucial to the success of government propaganda, which is one reason that political governments of all kinds insist that people learn to read. If government can then restrict what reading material is available, it can control what people learn and, to some extent, what people think. Some governments discovered that the outright prohibition of a book is a sure way to create a market for it, so they take the alternative strategy of destroying an author's reputation or ignoring an author's existence before a potential market becomes curious; this has been the academic, publishing, and media strategy for decades—Ayn Rand's work became widely known and respected despite the best efforts to suppress it or to ignore it, a remarkable exception.

The Internet changes everything. Writers can reach a vast number of anonymous individuals with any conceivable idea across national boundaries whether governments like it or not—and governments don't like it at all. All nation-states are struggling to impose restrictions on Internet content and Internet communications, something they can do only with the cooperation of people educated and skilled in information technology. Can governments force high-tech people to cut their own throats? We'll see. Meanwhile, writers who oppose government are pumping out more and more content every day and people are reading it and thinking about it. Individually, writers are taking a tremendous personal risk by exposing and defying the leviathan police states on this planet, states that could easily and perhaps joyfully plunge mankind back into the Dark Ages where they can rule as they would like to rule. Telling the truth is worth the risk and maybe, just maybe, the truth will help mankind survive.

# Propaganda

## 2001

Some say that this is my propaganda, my own spin on history and on
current events, and that it isn't true. Some say that the state is a
maligned benevolent benefactor of mankind. I reply that I would like to
see some evidence for that assertion. I claim that the state has no
money it does not steal. Show me the money that the state earns. The
state spends trillions of dollars every year. Where does that money
come from? It comes from taxes. Does the state earn taxes? No, the
state is not creating and selling goods and services that people may
freely buy or not buy on an open competitive market. Taxes are stolen
from people who earn their money. How are taxes stolen? Taxes are
stolen on goods at the point of sale. Taxes are factored into the cost of
services and are also stolen at the point of sale. Taxes on real estate are
stolen as a "quitrent" to the state annually; quitrents are an ancient
fraud based on the principle that all property belongs to the state. Taxes
on income are stolen via the employer and corrected annually by the
individual or stolen directly from the individual. Taxes on estates are
stolen directly by government agents after the individual dies. A person
is taxed from before birth until after death; there is no escape. Is this my
propaganda or is this the truth?

Let's ask why people permit this theft? I have heard people offer some answers over the years. "I pay taxes because I want to." "I pay taxes because it's fair." "People should pay for their government." "American taxes are too low, you ought to see what the (Germans, French, British, Canadians, etc.) pay." We have a picture here of a benevolent public voluntarily paying taxes to their benevolent government for the services that government provides to the public. I have to admit that this is a widespread and popular notion, but is the notion founded on fact or on fantasy? What service does political government provide to the people?

When I have politely inquired what people think of first when they think of government, the answer is usually police, with the fire department running a close second. People want security in their persons and in their property and they expect their government to provide it. Does government provide security? In a sense it does, while in fact it doesn't. The existence of community police and fire departments assures us that they are there if we need them, but we only need them during or after some violation of our security; their existence does not prevent the violation, therefore their existence does not provide security. Could some other institution actually prevent a violation of security? Yes, insurance could, but not the kind of insurance that is available today.

When I have asked further questions about the need for government, people usually respond that they expect government to provide justice, that is a system of reasonable laws that define and regulate human behavior as judged by the courts. Presumably, the legislature writes these laws, the executive endorses them, and the courts use them as the rules to follow in judgment of a given issue. Outside of traffic tickets, most people have little or nothing to do with this legal system, yet we are vaguely assured that justice exists—television fiction writers tell us it does. Does political government provide justice? In the light of real events and without writing another book on the subject, I feel safe in answering, no, it does not (the O.J. trial comes to mind). Could some other institution actually provide justice? Yes, insurance could, but not the kind of insurance that is available today.

I want to live in a society where individuals are not motivated to lie, cheat, and steal by any possibility of success, where if they do so they are motivated to pay for their crime. I want to live in a house that cannot be destroyed by fire, flood, earthquake, or hurricane. I want to move about in a vehicle that cannot fail or crash into another vehicle. I want to communicate in total privacy and secrecy. Are these impossible dreams? Certainly not, the technology already exists to provide what I want. Can government provide these things? Certainly not, it is political government that prevents them from happening; government has its own interests to protect.

What about war? War is the use of force between political governments; without political governments, there can be no war. So what is the issue at stake when people claim to fear war if political government ceases to exist? There seems to be a logical contradiction in the question. The reality is that we know of no other history of mankind than of political governments and their taxes and their wars and to imagine a human society without them is close to impossible. To many people the idea is not even desirable because their own self-interest is embedded in the monopoly on force that is political government, i.e., many people benefit from the redistribution of wealth at gunpoint. Naked coercion is cloaked in many disguises, however, which makes denial of the gun simple and easy.

I used to wonder how many people worked for the state and were thus direct beneficiaries of the systematic and organized theft that is taxation. I soon realized that this is the wrong question. The correct question is, how many people do not work for the state and are not the indirect beneficiaries of this crime? Perhaps an Eskimo here or there; the number is very close to zero. Somewhere between sixty and eighty percent of the wealth produced annually is funneled through political government on its way back into the general economy; everybody pays and everybody benefits, though some special interests may benefit more than others and the concomitant government regulations and costs are ignored. The process is so common and so generally accepted that people can easily deny that it is a criminal activity from start to finish.

The criminal nature of political government only becomes apparent when it applies its monopoly on the use of force against the people it is supposed to be benefiting, when its guns are drawn, aimed, and fired at its own citizens. The real tragedy at Wounded Knee, Kent State, Ruby Ridge, and Waco is that people refused to admit to themselves what these events really meant. If you defy your government, it will kill you.

Some individuals are foolish enough to refuse to pay income and/or property taxes; they resist the thieving criminals. We never hear much about them, but they do exist here and there. Government agents simply confiscate their property and/or throw them in jail, which is "justice" as determined in court. If they physically resist this "justice", they are murdered.

Community police forces are transforming into military assault forces under our very noses and people refuse to notice. Military combat forces carry out training exercises in our cities and suburbs and people refuse to notice. Political government is preparing for war in our towns and cities across the country and people refuse to notice. Against whom are these forces arrayed?

Hard telling. Americans go about their business and pay their taxes, as usual, and borrow money against future earnings to make up their personal deficits from taxation day by day. There are those who worry about the unimaginably huge pyramid of debt and taxes that flows through and sustains the American economy. It all depends on individual willingness to spend the energy of life on earning the money to pay the bills; it all depends on the personal selfish self-interest inherent in buying the goods and services a person wants and needs. There are those who worry about the demographics of this pyramid; if the numbers at the bottom stop growing, what happens at the top? Or if real wealth begins to vanish from the system, what happens to the whole structure? Will it collapse? Indeed, such a threat would bring out the armed forces all right. Is such a threat to be feared?

I believe the threat of collapse is built into the system of social organization we call political government, the nation-state or city-state or any state, a system that relies on the monopoly of the use of force to preserve its authority, i.e., the power to kill. Together with fraud, the force of political government is irresistible and its sole purpose is itself, a cancer feeding on the life of society. Why mankind has resorted to this doomed method of organizing society throughout history is no mystery, it perfectly reflects our human roots in nature as a violent, self-centered species, and no doubt we could go on for further millennia in our bloody mindless way except for two totally unanticipated and unprecedented changes in our circumstances as a species, our numbers and our technology—the two go hand in hand.

Homo Sapiens today confronts the ultimate dilemma of species success, self-destruction. We haven't eaten ourselves out of house and home, as predicted, because our science and technology saved us. We haven't died out from pandemic disease, as predicted, because our science and technology saved us. And we haven't yet precipitated nuclear winter, the species suicide that our science and technology put into the hands of political government. Is it only a matter of time? Who can predict?

Mankind must get past this juncture to survive. Mankind must eliminate the efficacy of force and fraud in human relationships, regardless of its origin in human nature. Mankind must go beyond political government to a system of social organization that promises durable success instead of inevitable failure. That means the creation of institutions that guarantee (not promise) security and justice without the use of force and fraud. These institution are already foreseeable, there is nothing mysterious about insurance and banking and the money-back guarantee, and our science and technology can provide the means to deploy and to access them throughout the planet. But old habits die hard, if they die at all, and coercion is a very old habit among us; to threaten the embodiment of coercion, the state, may itself be a fatal endeavor. Damned if we do, damned if we don't. Well, the ants won't miss us and the alligators will survive and new life-forms will emerge within the biosphere of this planet no matter what we do, although the prospect of human self-extinction does seem like a waste.

Here is my propaganda: that human beings in their various shades of physical and intellectual competence and in their various selfish desires will create their own best situation to get what they want with what they've got. There is no way around this, it is human nature. Human beings have tried to devise governments to provide security and justice within societies and these governments have always been modeled on the natural human recourse to physical force and intellectual fraud to create some hypothetical "best" situation for that society. Such government, political government, has always failed, that is 100% failure for all recorded history. We, mankind, cannot afford to fail again, we will not get another chance. It's time to try a different approach to government, an economic approach that actually appeals to individual selfish self-interest for success: to offer security and justice as products for sale with a money-back guarantee of satisfaction. Force and fraud become impotent and expensive behavioral options in economic government and even though these characteristics of human nature cannot be eliminated, the destruction they cause can be attenuated. Then Homo Sapiens can become a truly stellar species.

# Afterword

Werner von Braun always worried me. What motivates a man like that? When Einstein realized that the physics of his time could produce the ultimate technology of destruction, he used his influential reputation to warn the President of the United States that Germany could manufacture the atomic bomb first. The Manhattan Project was the result of his warning. But could Germany deliver the bomb? Possibly, as the United States later demonstrated by delivering the bomb with an old-fashioned aircraft to civilian targets in Japan, but realistically, Germany needed a rocket to deliver the bomb.

Of course, we all know now that Germany didn't have the bomb technology that it could have had, but it did have the rocket technology, thanks to Werner von Braun. Werner von Braun subsequently led the effort in the United States to create the ICBM. He was a brilliant man and a dedicated man, dedicated to his science and to his technology. He did not care where the money came from to build his rockets, he only wanted to build his rockets.

There is a singular blindness in that kind of dedication that worries me. Political governments today would be helpless to carry out their use of force without people like Werner von Braun. When I think about the ordinary men and women who go to work every day to build the weapons of massive murder and destruction, I wonder what motivates them. A paycheck? Is that all?

Look, I'm just a working stiff myself. I mean, I go to work, I do my job, I collect my pay, then I come home and do what I want to do, which is study and write. Much of what I do at work is stupid and probably not necessary, but at least I don't hurt anybody in the process and once in a while I actually help somebody who is sick to get better. How people can go to work knowing that what they do is designed to hurt other people mystifies me. How can they do it? Why do they do it?

The rockets and the nuclear bombs are there, in place, thanks to the genius of people like Werner von Braun and thanks to the people who built them for a paycheck, but today they won't work and they cannot be delivered to civilian targets without the genius and the work of specialists in information technology, that is computer experts and programmers. These people are educated, sophisticated, knowledgeable, well-paid and they know damned well what they are doing. I don't understand why they are willing to do it.

The women and men of genius and ambition have put the most destructive forces in history into the hands of psychopaths and morons. If mankind fails as a species, the guilt will lie with them, our very best. But this fate does not need to be, we still have time to retrench, to consider our errors, and to create a new way to organize our society. I hope that we choose to do so.

As for me, I am only a minstrel singing another man's song. I will not live to see what happens, the future of mankind is up to you.

Other books by Robert Klassen:

Atlantis: A Novel about Economic
Government - ISBN 0-595-09482-1
copyright 1997

Death in America: Short Stories about
Terminal Illness and Death - ISBN
0-595-09610 copyright 2000